GARDEN
walls and floors

David Stevens

conran
OCTOPUS

First published in 1999 by
Conran Octopus Limited
37 Shelton Street
London WC2H 9HN
a part of Octopus Publishing Group

Material in this book was originally featured in The Garden Design
Sourcebook, published in 1995 by Conran Octopus Limited.

ISBN 1 84091 049 6

Illustrations by Vanessa Luff

Art Editors Tony Seddon, Amanda Lerwill
Project Editors Kate Bell, Tanya Robinson
Picture Research Nadine Bazar, Julia Pashley, Rachel Davies
Illustration Visualization Lesley Craig
Production Julia Golding, Julian Deeming

Printed in Hong Kong

CONTENTS

Good garden design is essentially simple and fit for its purpose. Great gardens inevitably display these qualities but in addition they relate to the house they adjoin, and the settting in which they are placed.

In broad terms, a garden is a delicate balance between an initial framework that defines and divides the space, and the subsequent features, ornaments and planting that bring it alive.

The bones or 'hard landscape' of a garden not only offer shelter and division in the form of walls, fences and screens of different kinds, but also provide the floor and other paved surfaces.

While most of these are indeed 'hard', we should not forget the potential of plants to form hedges, areas of ground cover and of course lawns.

Any project, inside or outside the home, inevitably involves financial outlay, but in terms of gardens, it will be the paving and walling that take the lion's share of a budget, quite possibly up to three quarters of the total cost.

Over the past few years, gardening and garden products have become big business, and you only have to observe the enormous array of paving, walling and fencing available at any garden centre, nursery or builders' yard to see how easily over-complication, which is the antithesis of good design, can become a problem.

We are seduced by what catches our eye, and it is little wonder that so many gardens end up as an unrelated mass of materials and ideas, rather than as well thought-out, simpler designs.

The problem is largely an historical one. Once whole areas were built and laid out in vernacular style, using only local materials, producing a feeling of harmony. Only recently have modern transportation systems allowed intrinsically heavy materials to be moved around easily. Fine stone or hand-made brick from one area can end up in a garden in quite a different locality, and although it looks superb in its own setting, it may appear decidedly uncomfortable in its new surroundings.

Many of today's materials are much more durable than traditional ones, as well as being cost-effective and good to look at, which all

means that the dividing line between a restrained, sensible choice, and the introduction of too many varied elements, is all too narrow.

However, such a wide range of available materials can be a positive asset. You can mix and match materials, but to do so effectively you must understand their characteristics, the way they relate to each other and particularly their relation to the adjoining house.

In some gardens the choices will be obvious. No one, I hope, would think of laying blue and red pre-cast concrete paving slabs outside a fine old stone cottage. The logical choice here would be a similar stone, a matching gravel or perhaps a mellow brick, depending on what is used locally. All these materials are of a kind, and as they belong to the same generic and visual family, they look and feel comfortable together.

Problems arise when there is no strongly defined local indentity – in the heart of a town where building styles from different eras may sit side by side. Yet even here there will be guidelines.

Above: *Simplicity is the key to good design With its strong Japanese overtones, this garden has impeccably styled floor, walls and decking.*

Opposite: *Walls provide boundaries that are both visually and physically strong, while a mix of local materials ensures character. An archway gives a glimpse of what lies beyond.*

Above: *In this excellent garden composition stability and continuity are combined in both the hard and soft landscape materials, and in the superb use of perspective.*

Above: *It is frequently the inherent characteristics of the site, and the position of a feature within the garden that will be the major factors in determining the final appearance of a particular area. This three-layered boundary displays tremendous strength of purpose.*

A rendered concrete and colour-washed suburban building might look fine with crisp grey paving and well-detailed raised beds built from disused railway sleepers; a dark courtyard in town might successfully be floored with reflective white chippings, teamed with polished black slate. Such settings could be contained by fences or other well-defined boundary treatments.

The really important lesson, which needs to be kept in mind at all times, is how to use and respect the materials at your disposal, so that they relate to one another, to the garden as a whole and to the setting at large. By doing so, you will ensure that the overall design is coherent.

In other words, my role in this book is to ensure that you get the materials and details right before you start. When these crucial decisons have been made, you will have all the tools you need effectively to implement your own ideas. Once the mechanics of garden design are understood, the rest will follow naturally.

Above: *Tension, mystery and surprise are key elements in garden design and an area that can be seen in its entirety at a single glance is far less attractive than one that is divided into different spaces, each with its own individual character. A curving path that disappears from view always provides a delicious invitation to explore beyond.*

KEY TO SYMBOLS

COST

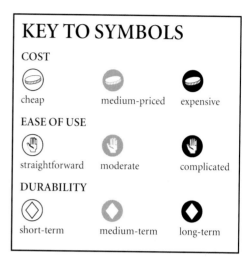

cheap   medium-priced   expensive

EASE OF USE

straightforward   moderate   complicated

DURABILITY

short-term   medium-term   long-term

Below Gravel is a good foil for architectural planting, such as the deep red swords of this Phormium tenax. The surface is continued from the path up into the shallow concrete steps, creating a subtle transition to another level.

Above: *The invitation to step outside should be strong and the elements here, from the decked porch, which links with the floorboards inside the house, to the carefully chosen weathered seat, achieve that ideal. The subtle relationship between the paving and planting provides a comfortable balance that is characteristic of much good design.*

Opposite: Floors can be simple or subtle, geometric or random. Here, the grid of stone strips frame the regularly clipped hedges to provide a solid but fascinating rhythm.

Left: A patchwork of broken paving materials gives an inherently 'busy' design. This path, however, is so well laid, with its carefully chosen stones and impeccably laid pieces of tile, that the whole composition becomes a work of art.

Below: To be effective, floors need to be well laid and visually attractive. In this composition, a simply planted bed, exposed aggregate slabs and bands of carefully laid cobbles are enclosed in a framework of brick paving.

The floor, whether formed of hard or soft landscaping, is one of the most important elements of a garden, often acting as a framework to the entire composition. Paving of various kinds will provide paths, steps, ramps, driveways, room for sitting and dining, as well as many other incidental features.

In terms of cost, a hard landscape floor will be a major investment, so it makes sense to decide with care and to ensure that it is laid or built to last. Any choice should be determined by the basic design and character of the garden, which will, in turn, be influenced by the style, location and age of the house it adjoins, as well as your own personality and lifestyle.

As with all aspects of design, there are definite guidelines that will suggest the right approach. For example, a brick house might well encourage a terrace of brick paving, teamed with pre-cast concrete slabs. Decking, on the other hand, may be ideal fronting a largely timber building, or useful on a steep slope, where interlocking platforms on different levels can be constructed.

While a single surface can appear visually 'heavy', three or more materials used together will almost certainly be too 'busy'. Two, in balanced proportions, however, will often look just right.

Larger impersonal spaces, such as driveways or parking areas, are more restful if constructed from a single material, such as gravel, concrete blocks or brick paviours. These will need containing or edging in some way, but elaborate or complicated edgings can impinge on the overall design, so remember to keep things simple.

While the finished look of any hard landscaped area is important, so too is the way in which it is constructed, as this will guarantee a long life and ensure safety – poorly laid slabs, for example, can be dangerous as they invite accidents.

Consequently, sound foundations are essential and these will range from something relatively simple, for heavy materials such as paving stones or railway sleepers, to a more solid, constructed base for smaller modules that move easily or that must sustain heavy wear and tear.

Drainage is another consideration and any surface should slope or 'fall' away from the house, usually with a minimum gradient of 1:100.

Although paving is usually used on a single plane, virtually all the options I shall be looking at will be equally suitable for steps and ramps – important in a sloping garden. Close to the house they may well be architectural in design while further away informality can be more appropriate.

Bearing in mind the cost of hard landscaping, large areas can often be given over to a softer treatment, and although this will take rather longer to establish, it will usually be far more cost-effective over time. To really make the most of soft surfaces, sound preparation, in the form of good topsoil and thorough cultivation, is essential. Whether such surfaces are grass, low ground-covering plants that form a carpet, drifts of wild flowers or sweeps of bulbs, will depend on their position within the overall design.

In the final analysis, you should always remember that the floor must provide a suitable background for a wide range of activities. It should not dominate the design, but should rather provide a subtle understatement, into and around which the boundaries and planting of the garden can be woven.

NATURAL STONE

Characteristics: Natural sandstone, of which York stone is a typical example, is found all over the world. It displays a wonderful range of subtle colours and textures, and it is this variation that makes it one of the finest and most sought-after paving materials. It is generally expensive.

Uses: This fine paving stone is perfect for seating areas, paths and terraces. It can be supplied new, sawn into slabs of virtually any size, or second-hand, when it is often reclaimed from street pavements or the floors of old mills and factories. If you choose the latter, check it carefully, as it may contain oil that will sweat out in hot weather, resulting in an oily mess.

From time to tome natural stone is available in very thin slabs, but these are likely not to be adequately durable for use outside. Broken stone, because of its inherently 'busy' nature, is best used in informal parts of the garden, or contained within a grid of brick or granite setts.

Laying: Slabs are normally supplied in random-sized rectangles, ranging from 900 x 600mm (36 x 24in) to 300 x 300mm (12 x 12in), and these should be laid around a small central keystone. Slabs will be of uneven thicknesses, and foundation levels must accommodate this. They should be bedded on a weak, semi-dry mortar mix to a minimum gradient of 1:100. They can either be neatly pointed, with the joints slightly rubbed back, or left open and filled with sifted soil so that low-growing plants can be seeded in the cracks. The occasional small slab can be omitted, and the space either planted, or infilled with a contrasting material – brick or cobbles, for example.

Contrasting & associating materials: Brick, granite setts, cobbles, gravel.

Natural stone quickly acquires a patina of age, with mosses and lichens colonizing the surface to produce a rich texture. The joints between slabs can be deliberately left open and filled with a little sifted soil, allowing plants such as alchemilla and verbascum to self-seed.

LAYING NATURAL STONE

Natural stone differs in size and thickness. Compensate by laying slabs on varying depths of mortar over a 100mm (4in) layer of hardcore.

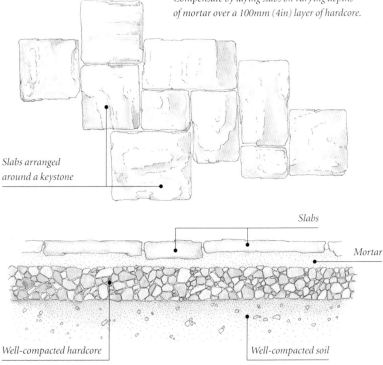

Slabs arranged around a keystone

Slabs

Mortar

Well-compacted hardcore

Well-compacted soil

These stone steps have an informal character that is both rugged and physically strong. The gentle curve of the flight naturally provides a feeling of movement that draws you inevitably up towards the higher level.

Possessing a great feeling of permanence and displaying subtle colour variations, natural sandstone paving is the finest paving material you can lay. Random rectangular slabs are ideal for terraces and pathways, and although a naturally architectural surface, it can be amply softened by allowing adjacent planting to flop over the edges.

GRANITE

Granite setts provide a durable and informal paving material that is ideal for paths in many parts of the garden. Because of their small size, setts can easily be laid to a curve. If the joints are left open, low-growing plants can be allowed to colonize.

FULL SETTS LAID IN A STRETCHER BOND

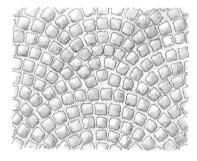

HALF SETTS LAID IN FAN SHAPES

LAYING GRANITE SETTS
To lay granite setts, bed them in mortar as tightly together as possible over a layer of compacted hardcore.

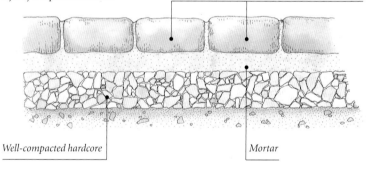

Tightly packed granite setts

Well-compacted hardcore   Mortar

Characteristics: Granite is a hard, igneous rock, found throughout the world. It is usually speckled in appearance, and can range in colour from pink, through brown to black. It has long been used in areas of heavy wear such as street paving, and was often laid in fan-shaped patterns.

Uses: Like sandstone, granite can be sawn into slabs, when it is incredibly expensive, but is more often seen as small rectangular paving blocks known as setts. Full setts are roughly the size of a brick; half setts are cube-shaped. Their surface is slightly uneven, making them ideal for paths, driveways, ramps and edgings, but less suitable for sitting areas.

Granite setts associate well with many other natural materials, and their small modular size allows them to be laid easily to curves or to form patterns. They can often be used as a frame for other materials, as edging for tarmac on a driveway, say, or to subdivide areas of brushed aggregate concrete. Setts are also effective used in courses around a tree or a smaller planting in an area of gravel.

Laying: Setts should be firmly set as closely as possible in a bed of mortar over a layer of well-compacted hardcore, and should be selected from the stack by hand, so that irregularities can be matched and minimized. If laying to a pattern, draw the pattern to scale first, marking any changes of direction, trims and other pertinent details. This will allow you to work accurately, and will help you to estimate the quantity of setts required.

Contrasting & associating materials: Sandstone, gravel; as trims or edgings, with concrete or tarmac.

Sawn and polished granite, although expensive, makes a superb paving material. Because of its great strength, it can be sawn into relatively thin tiles; the interlocking pattern shown on this roof garden produces a real feeling of movement.

SLATE

When split into small pieces and laid loose, slate can be used as a pathway or ground cover. Like gravel, it crunches loudly underfoot, giving it the added advantage of being a useful burglar deterrent. Here it is used successfully in a naturalistic setting.

Characteristics: Slate is a sedimentary rock found throughout the world. It is usually dark grey in colour, and splits easily along its bedding plane.

Uses: Slate is an ideal paving material. The dark colour associates well with lighter materials: when wet it becomes glossy, throwing it into sharper relief. However, it also absorbs heat, which can make slate paving alarmingly hot for bare feet! Slate can be sawn into rectangles to produce a crisp, finish; broken into 'crazy' or 'random' pieces which can be carefully laid and pointed; or broken into even smaller pieces and used loose as pathways, or as ground cover for plantings to grow through. Roof slates can be set on edge as paving, and although expensive, the end result is superb. Slate is also used as coping for some traditional walls, as a damp proof course, or as a creasing course beneath coping, to prevent moisture percolating up or down garden walls.

Laying: Slate paving needs to be firmly bedded in mortar over a well-consolidated layer of hardcore or crushed stone, to prevent it snapping.

Contrasting & associating materials: Light-coloured chippings and gravel, pale-coloured pre-cast paving, pale-coloured bricks, stone paving.

MARBLE

This stunning example of intricate paving shows craftsmanship at its best. Square marble slabs are subdivided by tiny patterned tiles which are perfectly aligned with the surrounding edging. This kind of scheme needs to be carefully thought out before the work starts.

Characteristics: Marble is a relatively hard sedimentary rock with wide colour variations and a veined surface. Good-quality stone is often expensive and difficult to find, but in the right garden the use of marble can have an unusual and often stunning effect.

Uses: Conjuring up images of Roman and Greek temples, marble has been used for centuries to build sophisticated buildings. This high-cost, dramatic surface is best used as sawn and polished slabs in up-market architectural schemes, perhaps linked to a similar floor inside the house. Its reflective qualities and pale colour can help to brighten a dark area, but marble must be used with sensitivity to avoid vulgarity, particularly in the softer light of temperate countries. Broken marble, used as random or crazy paving, should be avoided as it appears messy and uncomfortable. Courses or panels of polished slate can be used to provide a superb, if glitzy, counterpoint to marble slabs.

Laying: Marble slabs are usually of an even thickness and should be bedded on mortar over a well-compacted layer of hardcore or crushed stone. They can either be butt-jointed as closely as possible, or laid slightly further apart with deeply raked joints to emphasize the surface.

Contrasting & associating materials: Slate or other dark stones, including dark grey pre-cast concrete slabs.

COBBLES & BOULDERS

The visual power of these huge boulders is immense and they offer the perfect counterpoint to the simple architecture and the thick rendered garden walls they adjoin. Large rocks can be difficult to move so it is best to incorporate them into your design where they are found.

LAYING A COBBLE PATH
Lay cobbles tightly together so that no mortar is visible between each stone.

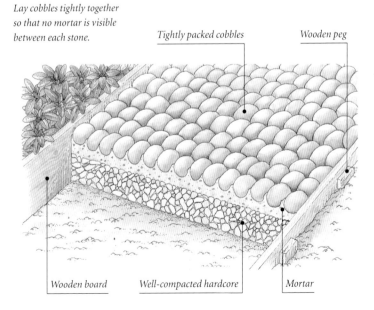

Tightly packed cobbles

Wooden peg

Wooden board

Well-compacted hardcore

Mortar

Characteristics: In general, cobbles are small and boulders large, but both are rounded, water-worn stones from river beds or the beach. (Incidentally, in many countries it is illegal for private individuals to take them away from the coast.) Cobbles and setts are often confused, but while setts are always rectangular or square, most cobbles are egg-shaped. Colour will vary, according to source, from almost black to white, through shades of blue-grey and pale grey.

Uses: Cobbles were, and in certain parts of the world still are, used for street and pedestrian paving, where they are often found in beautifully laid patterns. They form an uneven surface and are therefore ideal where grip is needed, on a sloping path or drive. They are, on the other hand, usually unsuitable for areas where furniture is likely to be used.

Cobbles usually look best laid as simply as possible, using a single colour and size, and packed as closely together as possible so that no mortar is visible between the joints. In larger paved areas, they can be used in panels or courses to form a contrast to other surfaces, to divide a space, or to surround and highlight a specific feature, such as a tree. Very small cobbles often look better than a large wedge of mortar between the joints of a curved path.

Laid loose, their character is completely different. Here, they can be piled up as a textured ground cover, either in areas where planting will not thrive, or as an excellent counterpoint to foliage. Difficult areas, such as manholes, can be easily disguised with a combination of loose cobbles, larger boulders and ground cover planting, all of which can be eased carefully out of the way if access is needed.

Boulders associate well with cobbles, and can provide sculptural interest too, if used in isolation. At their largest, perhaps a metre (several feet) in diameter, boulders can act as dramatic focal points, and can be positioned within a planted area or set in paving to act as occasional seats. Used in groups, they provide a physical deterrent, guiding both feet and eye through a space, or acting as a pivot at the turn of a path.

Cobbles and boulders associate particularly well with water. Cobbles can be used as a beach at the edge of a shallow pool or pond, and boulders can be drilled to allow water to flow up and over the surface. Both make far safer water features for children than an open expanse of water.

Laying: Where cobbles are to be walked on, they should be laid as closely together as possible, and bedded in mortar over a base of well-consolidated hardcore. If used loose, within a planted area, they can be placed over a base of weak concrete, black plastic sheeting, or a porous geo-textile. All these will prevent weeds growing up into the cobbles.

Boulders can either be laid loose, or bedded in mortar if they are set within a paved area where they are to be used for sitting, children's play, or as a sculptural feature.

Contrasting & associating materials: Both associate well with virtually any other surface, whether natural or man-made.

Cobbles are traditionally laid in intricate patterns which can engender a great sense of movement through an area. Here the pattern is reminiscent of a carpet and is carried in a long, elegant strip down the flight of steps, leading the eye round the corner of the building.

SAND

Raked sand in Japanese gardens is often used to represent a stretch of water. Here, large rocks are positioned in the sand to indicate islands in the middle of an ocean. This composition is a superb study in the texture of different materials.

Characteristics: The dividing line between gravel, grit and sand is a moot point; the finer gravel becomes, the closer it is to sand. Like gravel, sand comes in a wide range of colours and grades.

Uses: Fine sand is really only suitable for children's play areas, and 'silver sand' is the only satisfactory type even here; unlike the yellow builder's variety, it does not stain. The coarser types of sand may be used for a raked surface in gardens with a Japanese influence. However, the symbolism of Japanese gardens is probably best left to the Japanese, and it is generally more sensible to use a fairly straightforward pattern of raking rather than attempting to imitate the intricacies of the genuine article.

Laying: All sands and grits should be laid either over a weak mix of concrete or over a geo-textile membrane. The finished depth need not be great, 50–70mm (2–3in) is quite sufficient, but sand provides an ideal medium for the germination of weeds, and these will need to be attended to at regular intervals.

Contrasting & associating materials: Smooth, water-worn stones and boulders. Also looks superb with darker shades of timber decking.

GRAVEL, CHIPPINGS & HOGGIN

Characteristics: Gravel and chippings are both made up of small stones. As a general rule, gravel consists of rounded stones, while chippings are angular. Sizes vary from a few millimetres across, to approximately 12mm (½in). Hoggin is a binder consisting of clay and gravel extracted from the same pit, and is often used as a base for the first two, or by itself with a top-dressing of gravel. The colour and texture of these materials varies enormously.

Uses: These materials are frequently used for cost-effective paths and drives in both town and country. Being 'fluid', these materials can be laid in strong, flowing curves that give a real feeling of space and movement. The colour of the gravel or chippings can be chosen to link with adjoining stone- or brickwork, and paler colours used to reflect light in shady or dark areas – especially in urban basements or courtyard gardens. Gravel and chippings can provide a natural foil for planting allowed to grow through the surface, and will act as a mulch, retaining moisture in the ground.

Laying: The way in which gravel or chippings paths and driveways are laid is critical; a surface that is a struggle to walk across or washes about when driven over is quite unacceptable. Well-constructed surfaces that are firm underfoot can last over a hundred years but two things are essential: thorough compaction at every laying stage and edge restraints that prevent the surface from moving outwards. Edging can range from timber

boards, firmly pegged in position, to bricks haunched (set) in concrete.

Laying a driveway is best left to a professional, who will ensure that the foundation and base course use the correct size of stone and that it is thoroughly rolled. Foundations for a driveway, which takes more wear than a path, need to be a minimum of 150mm (6in). The top wearing course of hoggin is laid to a slight camber so that it sheds water easily, preventing puddles forming, which would quickly undermine the surface. The final top dressing of gravel will be just enough to cover the surface, and is rolled into dampened hoggin, which will act as a binder.

Gravel and hoggin paths are laid in much the same way, but with shallower foundations. Chippings are also laid over a firm and well-compacted base of crushed stone or hardcore, but the surface is left looser, to form a decorative element rather than a hard-wearing surface.

Loose gravel used as a foil to planting can be laid over a weak mix of concrete with gaps left for planting pockets, or over a sheet of geo-textile membrane which has been pierced to allow plants to grow through. Such areas can be allowed to run off into surrounding beds and do not need a firm edge restraint.

Contrasting & associating materials: All associate with the widest possible range of both hard and soft landscape surfaces and features; can be closely matched for colour, or used as a definite contrast (e.g. honey-coloured gravel with a golden sandstone; or white chippings in sharp relief to polished black slate).

White chippings make a useful ground cover and provide an attractive foil to planting, which can be allowed to grow through the surface. Their ability to reflect light means they can be invaluable when used to brighten a dark courtyard or basement garden.

LAYING A GRAVEL PATH

Always lay gravel paths to a slight camber to allow water to drain off easily. Thorough compaction is necessary at all stages of the job and firm edge restraints are essential.

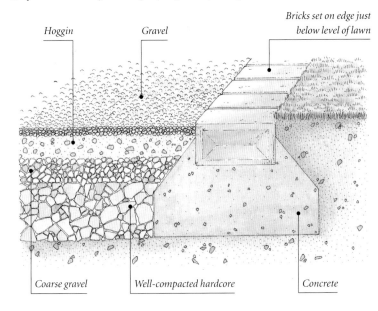

Hoggin

Gravel

Bricks set on edge just below level of lawn

Coarse gravel

Well-compacted hardcore

Concrete

This path is a pure work of art. It would take a great degree of determination to walk over the surface and disturb that beautifully raked pattern! It is an impeccable study in the contrast between different surfaces, the visual softness of the gravel complementing the stability and power of the natural stone slabs within a neat framework of grass.

DECKING

Characteristics: Timber decking is one of the most useful hard landscape materials available and, provided construction is carried out correctly, can be used anywhere in the world and expect a long and durable life. With the decimation of many tropical rain forests, it is worth checking that the timber comes from a renewable source.

Decking may be constructed from hardwood or softwood. Colours and graining provide a wonderful diversity of choice, and can be chosen to link with an adjoining wooden building or interior floor. Decking made from hardwood will need minimal maintenance, whereas softwood should be pressure-treated before it is used or treated regularly with non-toxic preservative.

Decking is a versatile material that is ideal for extending a horizontal surface out over a slope, in this case forming a roof terrace. Because timber is so easy to cut, it can be customized to fit the most awkward sites and shaped to fairly complex patterns. The timber theme can also be carried through the design to form handrails and other details.

CONSTRUCTING DECKING

Decking forms an ideal extension from the house, particularly when there is sloping ground. The direction of the boards will provide extra visual emphasis.

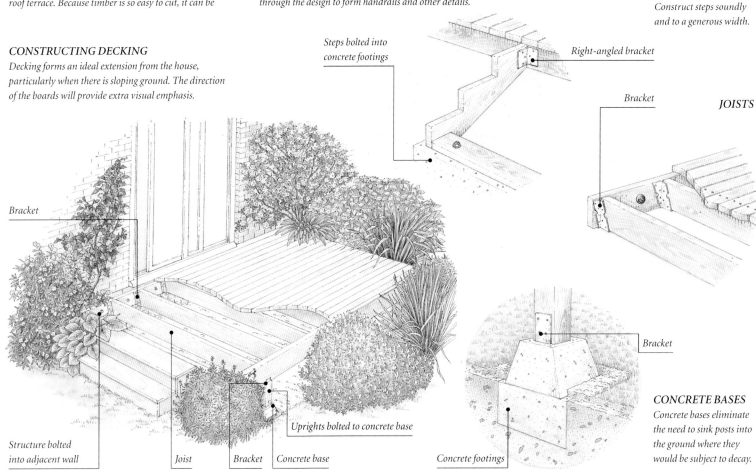

Steps bolted into concrete footings

STEPS
Construct steps soundly and to a generous width.

Right-angled bracket

Bracket

JOISTS

Bracket

Structure bolted into adjacent wall

Joist

Bracket

Concrete base

Uprights bolted to concrete base

Concrete footings

Bracket

CONCRETE BASES
Concrete bases eliminate the need to sink posts into the ground where they would be subject to decay.

Uses: Decking is particularly valuable where a garden slopes away from the house, enabling a series of decks, linked by steps, to provide flat surfaces adjacent to the building. Decks can also be used around water features or swimming pools, as barbecue areas, or to form boardwalks through woodland. Seats, rails, steps, overheads, tubs and other features can easily be incorporated as required. Decking is particularly well suited to sites where load-bearing is a problem, such as roof gardens and balconies. Additionally, it can be cut into virtually any shape, echoing the lines of adjoining architecture, or allowing established trees to grow through the surface.

Construction: Any competent carpenter can build decking, using straightforward skills. Adequate ventilation is essential, especially in wetter climates; there should be a minimum clearance from the ground of 150mm (6in). A framework of joists is bolted to uprights concreted into the ground. Boards are then nailed or screwed on to the joists, and a strong visual emphasis can be determined by the direction in which these boards run in relation to the house or immediate surroundings. Wide boards tend to make a space feel smaller, whereas narrow ones make it feel larger. Boards of different widths set up an interesting rhythm. Whatever their size, make sure spacing is regular, and not so wide as to trap spike heeled shoes.

On a roof garden, a lighter supporting framework of 50 x 50mm (2 x 2in) timbers is set on shims (thin wedges) to level the surface, and care must be taken not to obstruct drainage. Boards are then nailed to the framework, and these can be set diagonally or at right angles to the main building, or in small chequerboard panels.

Contrasting & associating materials: A house built of the same material, woodland settings, and timber such as railway sleepers; in a contemporary setting, decking looks handsome when placed near brushed aggregate paving, gravel, or *in situ* concrete walling.

Boardwalks make attractive features and are particularly successful when sited close to water, where they can be shaped to complement the curve of a bank. They should be set on solid timber piles driven into the surrounding ground. Water-resistant hardwood, such as elm, is ideal for the latter or, alternatively, you could use concrete posts.

Timber boards possess a strong architectural line that will draw the eye in a particular direction. They also weather beautifully, the slightly harder grain in the wood gradually becoming exposed and standing out in relief to form a rich surface patina. Timber furniture is the most logical choice for extending the theme.

RAILWAY SLEEPERS & LOGS

Logs can be used to form attractive and durable paths and steps, particularly in an informal or woodland setting. Remove any bark from the timber to minimize the chances of rot. Soften the line of the path by encouraging adjacent planting to flop over the edges. Additional planting can be seeded into the joints between each log.

Characteristics: Railway sleepers (known in the United States as railway ties) measure approximately 2.5m × 200mm × 130mm (8ft × 8in × 5in); logs may be any size. Either will form a powerful element in any composition. Sleepers are usually pine and, as they have been treated with preservative, rarely need any further protection. It is important to select clean sleepers, as many are contaminated with oil which may sweat out during hot weather. Logs can be hardwood or softwood and are usually untreated; however, it is possible to buy bark-stripped and pressure-treated logs of a specific diameter: these are regular in shape and more architectural in nature.

Uses: Railway sleepers make fine paths, steps, raised beds and paving, though the slightly uneven surface may not make them suitable for positioning tables and chairs. Both sleepers and logs can be used for steps; treads and risers can abut one another, or wider treads can incorporate a range of surfaces such as chipped bark, gravel, or – in a more architectural setting – paving of various kinds. Steps can be straight. or informally staggered, with planting softening the edges.

Laying/Construction: Because of the heavy weight of logs and sleepers, solid foundations are not usually necessary. For paving, a foundation of well-compacted soil is normally adequate. They should then be bedded close together on a 50mm (2in) layer of sifted soil to allow for levelling. No fall is necessary, as water can drain away freely between them.

For steps on a shallow slope, sleepers and logs can often be bedded directly into cut-outs in the bank. On a steeper gradient, it may be necessary to peg the risers with wooden stakes (set behind the risers to hide them) or to drill the timbers and drive metal rods vertically at least 600mm (24in) into the ground. Treads can be formed either from another sleeper, set behind the riser, or from another compatible surface. Where logs are used, they should have a diameter of at least 150mm (6in), and be firmly pegged in position. As edging for an informal path through a level area, the logs can be partially buried in the ground.

Contrasting & associating materials: Railway sleepers: virtually all other hard landscape materials, such as pre-cast concrete slabs, gravel, stone chippings or brushed aggregate, especially those in a contrasting colour. In less formal situations: chipped bark, gravel or hoggin.

Railway sleepers can be used to construct relaxed and easy-going steps that are ideal in an informal part of the garden. Well-compacted gravel is a good choice for treads and a series of terracotta pots have been used to reinforce the visual impact of the flight.

CONSTRUCTING LOG STEPS

Log steps are ideal in an informal setting. Risers of unequal lengths will merge naturally into any adjacent planting.

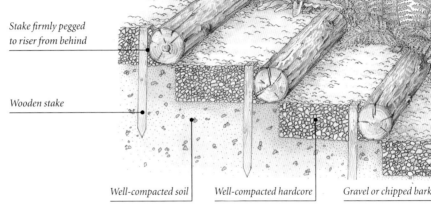

Stake firmly pegged to riser from behind

Wooden stake

Well-compacted soil

Well-compacted hardcore

Gravel or chipped bark

LOG SLICES

Log slices of an irregular size can be laid to form a rich, almost abstract, surface texture that is full of interest. These have been bedded into a layer of fine gravel, the pale colour throwing the timber into sharp relief.

Characteristics: Log slices consist of discs sawn from the trunks of trees. Hardwoods are the best choice as they last longest. Slices need to have a minimum diameter of 450mm (18in) and to be at least 150mm (6in) thick.

Uses: Usually laid informally as stepping stones through a wild area, through woodland or through planting, log slices can sometimes be used to form an informal paved area, butted together as tightly as possible, with wood chips filling the joints.

Laying: Log slices are laid directly on to soil excavated to a depth of 150mm

(6in) before being levelled and compacted. Lay stepping stones on the ground and try out the distance between them for comfort before bedding them in. Staggering the line of the path creates the most naturalistic effect. If the area is shady and the wood likely to become slippery as a result, you can staple chicken wire to the surface to improve the grip.

Contrasting & associating materials: Usually best on their own, or to link areas of wooden decking or railway sleepers; associate well with wood chips and gravel.

Natural materials blend perfectly into a natural situation and always look far better in such places than pre-cast concrete slabs or natural stone. Provided they are sufficiently thick, hardwood slices will last a remarkably long time.

CHIPPED BARK

The informal character of chipped bark makes it ideal for constructing low-cost and surprisingly durable paths in a naturalistic setting. It associates particularly well with planting but a certain degree of ongoing maintenance will be necessary to eliminate weeds.

Characteristics: Chipped bark is becoming increasingly popular. Bark is ground down to produce chips ranging from large 75 x 75mm (3 x 3in) pieces, to a finely chopped mulch. The chips can be used as a ground cover over large planting areas. The mulch, while ideal as a top dressing, rots down too quickly to be used on paths or play areas; use chips 12–25mm (½–1in) in diameter for these. Never use diseased wood, but any species of timber is suitable.

Uses: Fine chippings can be used as a water-retentive and weed-suppressing mulch around plants; coarser chippings are better for surfacing steps, paths, ramps, informal sitting areas and play areas, where they are easy on the knees and overcome the problem of worn grass.

Laying: As a mulch, about 70mm (3in) of finely ground bark should be laid over ground that has been cleaned of perennial weeds. For paths and sitting areas, approximately 25–50mm (1–2in) of coarser bark should be laid over well-compacted soil. Play areas require a thick 70mm (3in) covering of coarse bark laid on geo-textile membrane over well-consolidated ground. Chippings can usually be allowed to 'drift' into planting alongside; if an edge restraint is necessary or desirable, railway sleepers, logs or boards can be pegged firmly into position.

Contrasting & associating materials: Other timber surfaces, such as railway sleepers, wood slices, log steps, edgings and decking in informal parts of the garden.

Finely chipped bark provides an ideal mulch both around and below planting. Ample depth is necessary – at least 5–7cm (2–3in) – as the surface will slowly degrade, adding extra organic material to the ground. Topping up is therefore required every two or three years.

PRE-CAST CONCRETE PAVING

Pre-cast concrete paving is the workhorse of many a hard landscaping scheme and is best used as a simple, no-nonsense background that is suitable for a wide range of activities. Concrete slabs should never be allowed to dominate a scheme. Areas of terracing should be laid to a slight slope to allow water to drain off adequately.

Characteristics: There is a huge range of pre-cast concrete paving available today. Good-quality slabs are probably the best and most economical form of reproduction stone paving you can buy, and if laid properly should last a lifetime. They come in many different colours and in a wide variety of textures, so you will need to be strong-minded when choosing. In general, brightly coloured slabs are best avoided; they rarely link with their surroundings, and the colours often fade. Slabs in shades of grey, which blend well with virtually any setting, or those which echo the pale honey-yellow of natural yellow sandstone are by far the best.

Surface textures range from polished aggregate that successfully imitates granite or marble, to coarser, heavily textured aggregates, smooth concrete, or imitation natural stone. Many imitation stone slabs are of poor quality and should be avoided, but some are almost indistinguishable from the real thing – at about half the price. Remember that the more heavily textured the surface, the more uneven it will be for tables and chairs, though it certainly provides excellent grip for paths.

Uses: Paving provides a background for a wide range of activities, and it is important that the colour and pattern of the slabs do not dominate. It works best with one other surface material; used with brick, for example, an effective visual link can be made with an adjoining building, which will soften the overall effect.

The pattern in which slabs are laid can also play an important role in the overall design. Square slabs laid in a simple grid tend to be static; the same slabs set to a staggered or breaking bond will produce a greater feeling of movement. Rectangular 600 x 300mm (24 x 12in) slabs laid across a space in a staggered bond will draw the space apart and make it feel wider; laid down a terrace or path in this way, they will accelerate the view and possibly foreshorten the space. Random rectangular paving creates the least formal pattern, while paving using broken slabs will be visually unsettling close to a building, unless contained within a strong framework of another material such as brick or granite setts.

Slabs can also be used for steps, ramps, stepping stones across lawns or through planting, and as broad coping, doubling as occasional seats, on the top of low walls or raised beds.

Laying: As with all paving, the correct laying of concrete slabs is essential. Bedding them on sand is a short-term option that quickly leads to trouble: the surface will become undermined and the slabs uneven. The standard method is to lay a firm base of well-compacted hardcore or crushed stone, and bed the slabs on five spots of mortar – one under each corner and one in the middle. For a driveway, or anywhere likely to get heavy wear, slabs should be bedded on a continuous layer of mortar on a firm base. Any paving should be set to a slight fall away from the house, or into gullies.

Check the position of drains, manholes or other services, and never pave over or obstruct these.

Slabs can be either butt-jointed as closely together as possible, or laid with a slight gap between them, which is subsequently pointed. The pointing can be flush, rubbed back or raked out; a deep, raked-out joint will create shadow, emphasizing the surface pattern. It is also possible to butt-joint courses of slabs, and rake out the joint to either side. This results in a strong directional emphasis that can be useful in certain design situations.

Stepping stones can be bedded on a weak mortar mix over well-compacted ground, but ensure that the slabs are just below the surface of a lawn, to allow for easy mowing.

Contrasting & associating materials: Nearly all surfaces, hard or soft, because of the range of pre-cast concrete paving available.

This is an excellent example of a well-made concrete slab that simulates natural stone. The surface is not too heavily textured and the slabs have been perfectly laid. Although this is a random pattern, the courses run across the path, and these, together with the bands of brick, help to widen the space, linking it with the planting on either side.

Exposed aggregate slabs have an attractive, rugged surface texture that provides both grip and visual interest, and which can often provide an excellent foil to planting. The central joint of this path tends to draw the eye, which has the effect of accelerating the view.

BRICK

Brick is a warm, mellow and immensely useful paving material that can be laid in a wide range of patterns. Because of its small unit size, it can be laid to curves and can often be employed to extend a surface into awkward spaces without the need for any cutting.

LAYING A BRICK PATH

To lay a brick path, either bed the bricks in a wet mortar mix, or in a semi-dry mix which is subsequently dampened down. Sound edge restraints are essential.

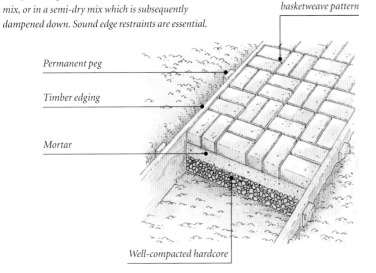

Permanent peg

Timber edging

Mortar

Well-compacted hardcore

Brick laid in basketweave pattern

Characteristics: Brick is one of the finest small modules available for paving; it is available in a vast range of colours, finishes and densities, and can form the perfect link with a house built of the same material. It is important to check with your supplier that what you have chosen will stand up to winter frost; some older bricks break up easily.

Manufacturers are now producing an increasing range of brick 'paviours' specifically for paving. Stable paviours have patterned surfaces, often like that of a bar of chocolate, or impressed with a diamond pattern, and are effective used as a contrast within another surface, or alone for paths or drives where a good grip is important.

Uses: Brick can be used for virtually any kind of paving, but its small size and often dark colour can make it look heavy if used alone over large areas. Laying patterns include herringbone (the most complicated), basketweave, stretcher bond and soldier courses; all are more or less demanding on the eye. Once again,

the laying pattern determines the emphasis: where stretcher bond leads the eye on, basketweave produces a more static result.

Laying: All brick paving must be laid over a well-compacted base of hardcore or crushed stone. Bricks can then be bedded on a semi-dry mortar mix, with secure edge restraints at the sides of the path or paved area. Once the pattern has been set out, additional mortar should be carefully brushed into the joints, and the whole area lightly wetted with a fine spray. For a more durable finish, bricks should be bedded into a wet mortar mix, and the joints pointed when it is dry. This must be done with care, as shoddy pointing looks unsightly, and mortar on the face of bricks is extremely difficult to remove. Brick takes longer to lay than, say, natural York stone or pre-cast concrete slabs, and the cost of laying is therefore greater.

Contrasting & associating materials: Brick associates well with virtually all other materials.

LAYING PATTERNS

Lay bricks either flat, as shown here, or on edge. The latter method obviously uses a greater number of bricks.

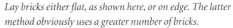

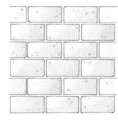
Stretcher Bond

Herringbone

Basketweave

This herringbone brick floor provides the perfect visual link with the surrounding high brick walls. Such a floor will have a long life if well laid, and its richly textured pattern is the ideal foil for formal planting.

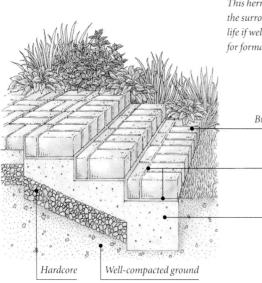

Bricks on edge

Mortar

Concrete

CONSTRUCTING BRICK STEPS

Always build steps to wide, inviting proportions. Sound concrete foundations are a necessity.

Hardcore   Well-compacted ground

As bricks are such small modules, they can be laid to strong flowing curves that lead both feet and eyes through a space. A stretcher bond has the strongest directional emphasis, and here this is reinforced by the dynamic planting to either side of the path.

TILES

Terracotta tiles often have a strong vernacular character that can make them the perfect choice in regional settings. Their mellow colour allows them to blend well with many other hard landscape materials, whether man-made or natural.

LAYING TILES ON EDGE
This is a superb pattern that was traditionally laid using slate rather than tiles. Set all surfaces in mortar over well-consolidated hardcore.

Brick edging set in mortar

Slate can be combined with tiles for a different effect

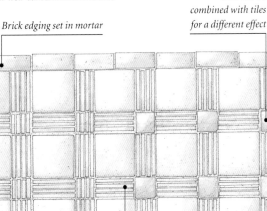
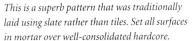

Tiles laid flat

Tiles set on edge

Humour is an indispensable part of good garden design and this garden positively oozes both fun and strong character. The deep blue, hand-made tiles link with the coping on the raised beds and pick up the blues of the pot. The arch is bursting with individuality.

Characteristics: Like bricks, tiles display a wide regional variation in colour, and not all are frost-proof; this should be checked with the supplier. Terracotta is the most common and the surface is usually smooth or slightly textured. Sizes vary from 300mm (12in) square down to 150mm (6in) square. A wide range of patterned glazed tiles is available, but most are too 'busy' for use in the garden.

Uses: Tiles are best suited to smaller, more intimate areas of the garden, where they can be used for paving, steps, or coping on low walls or raised beds. Terracotta tiles can provide a wonderful link with similar tiles inside the house. Roof tiles, like roofing slates, can also be set on edge to produce intricate and elegant paving patterns, a device often used by the architect Sir Edwin Lutyens in the early part of the century.

Laying: Tiles should be bedded in mortar over a base of smooth concrete, and tightly butted together.

Contrasting & associating materials: Tiles are best used on their own but can look effective when carefully integrated with slate or other paving.

CLAY GRANULES

CONCRETE BLOCKS

Clay granules provide an excellent mulch in pots or around larger areas of planting. They are particularly useful for use on roof gardens and balconies, where their light weight comes into its own. Their colour blends well with most surfaces, especially terracotta.

Concrete blocks can look much the same as bricks from a distance, but there is less variation in colour, which can make large areas of paving appear rather monotonous. They are best used, as here, in an area with interesting characteristics or features. This simple stretcher bond leads the eye down the path, reinforcing the line of the low hedges.

CLAY GRANULES

Characteristics: Lightweight clay granules, commonly used as a houseplant dressing or growing medium, have a diameter of approximately 6mm (¼in). The brown colour forms a neutral background that blends well with most plants and situations.

Uses: Where weight is an important consideration – on roof gardens, for example – clay granules can be used as a mulch around planting, or as an attractive flooring for parts of the roof that are not walked on, perhaps around a water feature or other focal point. They could be laid in swirling patterns combined with pale-coloured gravel or chippings.

Laying: Tip out of a bag and spread to a depth of about 50mm (2in) over virtually any surface.

Contrasting & associating materials: The neutral colour of the granules blends well with planting and most other hard landscape surfaces.

CONCRETE BLOCKS

Characteristics: Blocks are either approximately the same shape and size as bricks, or are irregular in shape, and interlock with one another to provide added strength. They come in a wide range of colours, including dark grey, red, pink and brown. While the surface is clearly concrete, an area paved with these small coloured modules is not unattractive and is also inexpensive and durable.

Uses: Best suited to driveways and other areas of heavy wear. Their rather monotonous colour and surface texture makes them unsuitable for terracing or intimate paved areas, even if they are cheaper than brick.

Laying: Concrete blocks must be butt-jointed and bedded on sand over a well-consolidated bed of hardcore or crushed stone. Once the blocks are put into place, more sand should be brushed into the joints and the whole surface compacted with a plate vibrator; this will allow the surface to flex slightly as traffic passes over it. A firm edge restraint is an essential requirement. Boards pegged into position are acceptable temporarily, but these will eventually deteriorate; best are special edging blocks set in concrete (generally available in a range of patterns to provide differing kerb details). The laying bonds used are usually herringbone or basketweave.

Contrasting & associating materials: Concrete blocks are usually best on their own, but can sometimes be used as panels within a contrasting pre-cast concrete slab.

IN SITU CONCRETE

In situ *concrete can provide a beautifully simple and neutral background on which a wide range of activities can take place. The warm colour shown here is produced by adding a dye to the mix, and links it perfectly with the colour scheme of the adjacent planting.*

Characteristics: *In situ* concrete is laid or cast on site. It can be laid to any shape, which allows for great flexibility of design, and the results can be both elegant and cost-effective. Concrete has been called the stone of the twentieth century. Used correctly, with flair and imagination, it is just that, and as its appearance depends on the aggregate (the small stones in the mix), the range of colour and finish on offer is enormous. Surfaces may be smooth, brushed with a broom, seeded with more small stones; exposed by careful washing down and brushing; ribbed; or tamped. Specialist companies will also add dyes to the mix, and impress the surface with patterns to imitate other surfaces. No one is fooled by these cheap imitations, however, and they are visually dishonest.

Uses: In many different situations, but especially with contemporary designs. It is also useful for free-form shapes where pre-cast concrete slabs would require cutting. The need to incorporate expansion joints can become a positive element in the overall design as the surface can be divided by strips of timber, paving slabs, brick or a range of other materials that can in turn be linked back to the house. An excellent, cost-effective choice for drives.

Laying: Must be laid over a well-consolidated base of hardcore or crushed stone. Panels of concrete must be no more than 3.6m (12ft) square, and divided by expansion joints to allow for expansion and contraction at different temperatures. These can be formed of strips of timber, paving slabs, brick, or any of a wide range of other materials.

LAYING IN SITU CONCRETE

In situ *concrete can be cast to virtually any pattern with a wide range of aggregate or other finishes.*

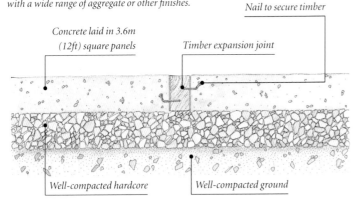

Nail to secure timber

Concrete laid in 3.6m (12ft) square panels

Timber expansion joint

Well-compacted hardcore

Well-compacted ground

ACHIEVING DIFFERENT FINISHES

Several different finishes are possible, including smoothing with a shovel for a slightly textured finish, brushing with a broom to expose the aggregate in the mix, or using a steel float for a smooth finish.

PLASTICS

Astroturf is best thought of as carpet rather than imitation grass. It provides an ideal floor in many situations, particularly roof gardens or around swimming pools. There is too much horticultural snobbery surrounding such surfaces: use them for what they are!

These no-nonsense concrete steps are both well-proportioned and well-constructed, linking with the concrete balustrade that borders the flight. Architectural planting plays an important role in softening the inevitable hard lines, while shadows add visual drama.

An edge restraint is only necessary as the concrete is laid and this can be used to make part of the overall pattern of expansion joints. If timber boards are used, these can be struck (removed) once the surface has dried out. The concrete itself should be approximately 70mm (3in) thick, and if an exposed aggregate finish is required, the stones chosen must be added to the ballast before the concrete is mixed. Other finishes can be implemented as the concrete is laid or drying out. In hot weather cover the surface with damp sacking or burlap to prevent it from drying out too quickly; if there is any danger of frost, it should be covered with plastic sheeting until completely dry.

Contrasting & associating materials: Best with other man-made materials, but some natural materials provide a good contrast for expansion joints.

Characteristics: Plastics have a great deal to offer. Plastic turf, known as Astroturf, is commonly used for sports fields; it is also useful on roof gardens or around swimming pools. It is light, durable, and comes in brown and black as well as green. Other industrial and sports arena floorings are now more widely available; they, too, are extremely durable, and come in a varied range of exciting colours and textures.

Uses: Plastic and other synthetic floorings can be used in any part of the garden, but are especially useful on roof gardens because of their light weight. They are particularly suited to contemporary, hi-tech settings. The large, flexible sheets can be cut to form strong, flowing curves, providing great fluidity in a design, and can be moulded over ramps, eliminating the need for steps in certain situations. The potential for mixing and matching dramatic swirls of colour, both outdoors and in, is exciting and limitless!

Laying: Plastic flooring must be laid, like vinyl flooring in the home, on a screed over a sound concrete base. It can sometimes be laid over existing paving. Whereas industrial flooring often needs to be fixed down with adhesive, Astroturf can simply be rolled out and cut to fit.

Contrasting & associating materials: Plastic and other synthetic flooring is best used on its own and usually works in a contemporary setting; it does not associate very happily with other hard landscape materials.

TRIMS & EDGES

Trims can play an important role in terms of design, and here the box hedge provides vertical emphasis while the polished slate stones beneath provide definition at a lower level. Neither of these elements provides a great degree of physical containment.

Good hard landscape is all about attention to detail, and one of the most important details is how to finish or retain surfacing materials. However, following the classic design rule of simplicity, edging should only be used if the surface actually needs it. You will often see an area of pre-cast concrete slabs or brick paving edged with a concrete kerb, a row of granite setts or cast rope edging. They are unnecessary and look fussy.

Surfaces which do need an edge or trim are usually 'fluid' – either permanently (e.g. gravel or wood chips) or temporarily until they set (e.g. *in situ* concrete or asphalt).

Some, such as concrete blocks, need an edge restraint to prevent the surface moving outwards and losing its integrity. Occasionally a trim can be used as a contrast to the main surface (e.g. natural paving or pre-cast concrete slabs edging a gravel or cobble path), but this must be an integral part of the design and not design for design's sake! Trims can also be invaluable as a mowing edge.

Many surfacing materials can be used as edges and trims: brick, granite setts, timber and pre-cast concrete slabs among them. Always suit the edging to the surface material and to the situation. A curving path

or driveway is best edged with small modules such as bricks or setts that will conform to the shape. Longer lengths of inflexible materials will form a visually uncomfortable edge.

Any form of edge must be securely fixed in position, either haunched in concrete, or, for timber, pegged into place, before the surface area is laid. Haunching consists of setting the edging in a concrete foundation that is chamfered away on the outside, allowing it to be covered with and hidden by soil, planting or grass. In the case of a mowing edge, slabs or bricks should be set in mortar or concrete just below the level of the turf. Although trims and edgings form only a small part of the cost of the surface you choose, check the details against the information provided for individual materials.

Brick: Bricks are immensely versatile and can be used with a wide range of surfaces. They are best laid on edge, either end to end, or side by side, which uses more bricks but looks more stable. The small brick modules allow you to cater for straight or curved runs, as well as surrounds for trees or planting. They also make an ideal mowing edge.

Concrete kerb edgings: These are cheap and much loved by builders. Unfortunately they look it! Approximately 900mm (36in) long and 230mm (9in) deep, they should be used only as a last resort, and then only for straight runs.

Granite setts: One of the most useful trims. Full or half setts can be used to edge gravel, chippings, brushed

aggregate, concrete or lawns. They will conform easily to curves, and can be used in a single, double or treble row for increasing visual emphasis. They can also be used within a gravel or hoggin area to form a surround for trees or other planting. Setts should be haunched in concrete.

Metal strips: Used in many established and historic gardens. Wrought-iron or steel edging strips provide crisp, no-nonsense trims that can look superb, particularly when retaining a slightly higher lawn at the edge of a drive. They can be used for straight or curved runs. These trims will last virtually for ever, but are expensive, often difficult to obtain, and their installation is a specialist job. Never confuse them with the flimsy corrugated alloy edging that can be bought in rolls from garden centres. This is barely strong enough to retain anything, will eventually get mangled in the mower (doing neither of them any good), and should be avoided at all cost.

Pre-cast concrete slabs: These can make a detailed edge for a wide range of materials, including gravel, hoggin, brushed aggregate or cobbles. The width and colour of the slabs should be chosen to fit in with the overall design of the garden. They are best for straight runs; slabs designed for curves should be studiously avoided because they exist only in set sizes and look terrible.

Rope edgings: Ever popular, these are available in cast concrete (which can look untidy), terracotta or stone. They look decidedly uncomfortable

Granite setts form a simple, no-nonsense and firm trim to many surfaces: in this case, an asphalt path. Planting can be allowed to flop over and soften the hard edges.

These traditional clay Victorian or Edwardian edgings are full of character, showing the patina and irregularities of age. Frost-proof engineering bricks act as a mowing edge.

Glazed terracotta 'rope' edgings are both elegant and durable – they should last for well over a hundred years – and they can form an ideal restraint for gravel paths.

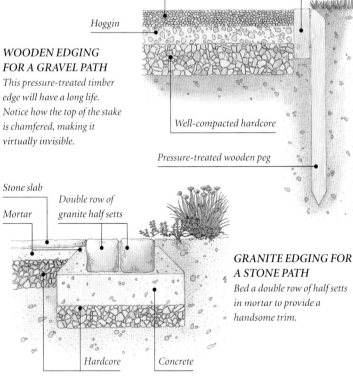

WOODEN EDGING FOR A GRAVEL PATH

This pressure-treated timber edge will have a long life. Notice how the top of the stake is chamfered, making it virtually invisible.

Gravel · Pressure-treated board · Hoggin · Well-compacted hardcore · Pressure-treated wooden peg

Stone slab · Mortar · Double row of granite half setts · Hardcore · Concrete

GRANITE EDGING FOR A STONE PATH

Bed a double row of half setts in mortar to provide a handsome trim.

in a contemporary setting, and are best used as a trim for a gravel or hoggin path. They must be set firmly in concrete to prevent movement.

Tiles: Laid side by side with just the edge visible, these form a delicate and intricate trim that can look superb in the right place. This effect requires a large number of frost-proof tiles, which should be set in mortar over a concrete foundation.

Timber: Boards, approximately 150 × 18mm (6 × ¾in), are the most cost-effective edging, and, being flexible, can be used to edge both straight and curved paths. Boards should be pressure-treated and pegged into position on the outside. Pegs 450mm (18in) long are hammered into the ground to just below the top of the boards, and the boards nailed to them.

Round sawn logs make an attractive informal edging, either placed in a trench and held in position with rammed soil, or set in concrete. They will easily conform to a curve. Unsawn logs make the most informal edging of all, and are perfect for a wood-chippings or rough grass path through woodland; heavy logs can simply be placed and left in position. Railway sleepers make a powerful edge for gravel, hoggin, cobbles or wood chips, but are only suitable for straight runs. They are heavy enough simply to lay on sifted soil over well-compacted ground.

Natural stone: A superb, traditional edging for straight, cobbled or gravelled paths. Strips approximately 300mm (12in) wide are set on edge, butt-jointed, and set in concrete to make a handsome mowing edge.

LAWNS

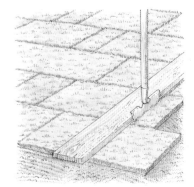

For a straight edge, cut along the edge of a board using a half-moon edger.

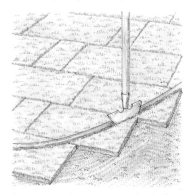

Set out curves from a predetermined point, with a fixed radius, and mark with a hose or line, before you cut through the turf.

The design permutations for using grass are virtually endless. In this strongly geometric pattern the whole area dishes down towards the level central circle. The octagonal gravel paths and surrounding hedges emphasize the underlying shape, the latter providing screening and shelter at the highest level.

The greater part of your garden floor may well be given over to soft landscape in the form of grass, ground cover or planting. While planting is outside the scope of this book, grass and ground cover are very much part of a garden's overall design overall design and organization of space.

Chamomile, thyme and other ground-hugging plants can also be used as lawns, but good, old-fashioned grass is still the most valuable and cost-effective flooring available in the garden. It is tough, easy to lay, straightforward to maintain, and remains the most suitable surface for the widest possible range of activities. It also looks good, especially in a temperate climate, where it will thrive in the moist conditions. The kind of lawn you choose will depend on the appearance

you wish it to have, and the level of maintenance you are prepared to undertake.

Grass lawns can be either seeded or turfed. In general, a turfed lawn will establish itself more quickly than a seeded one, and the preparations for a seeded lawn are rather more critical. The quality of either will be determined by the type of seed mix. A lawn with a hard-wearing surface that will cope with the demands of children, dogs, sporting grown-ups and a social life, will need a relatively high percentage of tough, broad-leafed species of grass. That epitome of the English garden, on the other hand, the perfect 'bowling green' lawn, with its immaculate cylinder mower stripes, is made up from finer grasses. Such stripes have a powerful visual effect in a design. If a long,

narrow lawn is mown up and down its length, the shape is emphasized. Try mowing it across, or diagonally, to increase the visual width. The air of mystery provoked by a lawn disappearing around a curve or wing of planting can be reinforced by a mowing pattern that follows the shape of the lawn, producing a sense of space and movement.

Weeding, feeding and cherishing a lawn does undoubtedly improve it, but weed seed, especially in country areas, will continue to invade, and it may be wiser to tolerate a degree of weeds and tough grasses for the sake of a surface that will wear better and be easier to maintain. Avoid, too, cutting your grass too short, which inhibits growth and allows the lawn to dry out in hot weather; 12–25mm (½–1in) is ideal.

The combination of rough grass and wild flowers is simply delightful. To look at its best, however, a composition like this needs to be sited in an area that is large enough to allow the paths to curve away out of sight into the background.

Easy maintenance, or the reverse, will be affected by other elements too. Complicated lawn patterns make mowing difficult, and edging by hand is a chore. So work out a bold and simple ground plan that links the lawn with the rest of the garden pattern, and lay a mowing edge of brick or slabs that will allow the mower to run smoothly over the top, eliminating the need for hand edging and protecting plants.

Areas of rough grass: As a general rule, the further away from the house, the softer and looser the composition can become. Shorn sward can give way to rougher grass that will look ideal beneath fruit trees, and a path mown through rough grass is always a delight. Such an area can be naturalized with bulbs and even wild flowers – although wild flowers thrive in relatively lean conditions, and

rich, fertile garden soil may well encourage stronger grasses and perennial weeds at their expense. Do not be disheartened if your display does not quite match that of the wild flower lawns at horticultural shows! Grass like this needs cutting only three times a year: once after the spring bulbs have died down, once after the summer flowers have set seed, and once before putting the area to bed for the winter.

Alpines: Many of the mat-forming alpine plants can be used as charming carpets in areas that are not much walked on. They can be grown in cracks between paving slabs, helping to soften the look of the overall surface, or as a larger carpet, when sweeps of several different species can swirl and intertwine, setting up a delightful dialogue. Nearly all alpines need a free-draining, gritty soil and plenty of sun if they are to thrive.

Chamomile: Chamomile lawns have a long history. They do not need cutting and are wonderfully fragrant when trodden on. To cross a chamomile lawn and sit enjoying the scent on a fine summer's evening is one of the great pleasures of life. They are fine in formal areas

where traffic is light, but they do take a long time to establish, they do need constant weeding while establishing, and they cannot tolerate heavy wear. Non-flowering *Chamaemelum nobile* 'Treneague' is the variety to buy.

Soleirolia: S. soleirolii (syn. *Helxine soleirolii*) or 'mind your own business' is a tiny-leafed plant, often considered a rampant weed. As a filler in cracks between paving, or as ground cover, it forms a dense green mat of superb foliage, thriving in shade and impossible conditions. It will not survive heavy wear, and should be kept well away (if possible) from other planting or conventional lawns.

Thyme: Like chamomile, thyme will not tolerate heavy wear, and takes a while to establish. However, its natural ground-hugging character makes it an ideal carpeter, and its flower is a real bonus. Grow *Thymus serpyllum* and *T. doerfleri*, both deliciously fragrant when crushed underfoot. Or grow the plants in a reasonably deep tray, remembering to water them, to use for a thyme seat or a thyme table. The effect will be worth the effort, and will always provide a talking point.

Chamomile is a naturally ground-hugging species that quickly forms a fragrant carpet, although it will only be able to survive light wear. In this imaginative design, the rope pattern, set within the brick paving, has an enormous feeling of movement, which is reinforced by the equally fragrant lavender planted on either side.

GROUND COVER

Many plants, too tall to be classed with lawns, can still be used to form a horizontal carpet for the garden. These ground-cover plants will exclude weed growth, and can be used to reinforce the floor pattern while keeping maintenance to a minimum. There are many suitable species, but you will need to do your homework to check the soil type and aspect that they prefer, as well as their height and spread. Plant labels will often give you the information you need. Moreover, you should resist the temptation to overplant; many ground covers are rampant and knit together fast. As with any planting, sound preparation is the secret of success. Make sure that the soil is well cultivated, free from perennial weeds, and contains as much organic matter as possible.

The following is not a comprehensive catalogue, simply a selection of available plants.

Ajuga reptans: There are a number of different bugles; 'Atropurpurea' is one of the best. Suitable for sun or part-shade, all are ground-hugging and not too invasive.

Bergenia: Large, rounded evergreen leaves, and pink or white flowers in spring. Excellent ground cover for sun or shade, and tolerant of a wide range of soils. *B. cordifolia* and its cultivars are the most suitable.

Cistus x *dansereaui* 'Decumbens' (syn. *C.* x *lusitanicus* 'Decumbens'): A wide-spreading, evergreen rock rose, ideal in full sun. The delicate white flowers are patterned with a crimson blotch at the centre.

Cotoneaster x *suecicus* 'Skogholm': Low, ground-hugging, excellent in sun or partial shade. Bears a profusion of red berries in the autumn.

Epimedium: Neat, low growers with small, heart-shaped leaves and delicate pink, white or yellow flowers on wiry stems. This is ideal in shade, and although it is reasonably quick to establish, it should not be too invasive.

Low-growing ground covers, for example moss and Soleirolia, are ideal in damp, shady conditions, such as those found beneath trees. They need little attention, apart from keeping them moist in dry weather. In this situation, the visual dialogue with the loose cobbles is an interesting one, both surfaces producing complete carpets.

Euphorbia: Many of the lower-growing spurges make good ground cover. *E. polychroma* is deciduous; *E. amygdaloïdes* var. *robbiae* semi-evergreen. Both have lime-green flower heads, and both are best in sun or partial shade.

Geranium: There are many herbaceous geraniums or cranesbills, varying in flower colour and in height from 60–90cm (24–36in) to semi-prostrate. The majority make superb ground cover and most like sun, though *G. endressii* thrives in shaded, open areas.

Hebe pinguifolia 'Pagei': A fine, low-growing, ground-covering hebe, with white flowers and glaucous-grey foliage. This does well in sun, and it thrives for me in light shade.

Hedera: Nearly all the ivies make terrific ground cover, and are one of the best plants to choose for shaded areas. They have the added advantage of being capable of running up any vertical surface that gets in their way. Most are fast-growing and invasive. There is a wide range of leaf shape, size, colour and variegation to choose from.

Hosta: No garden is complete without hostas. They thrive in sun or shade, have a vast range of leaf colour, and knit together without being rampant. All are deciduous.

Hypericum calycinum: Perhaps the best known of all ground covers, the rose of Sharon displays both the advantages and disadvantages of this group. This low-growing evergreen carries yellow buttercup flowers throughout the summer, and enjoys sun or shade. It is extremely invasive and needs to be confined, or cut back rapidly should it invade other areas.

Lamium: The much-maligned 'dead nettle' makes an excellent choice in full or partial shade. Strong-growing, and therefore best where it can be contained, it is ideal under trees. *L. maculatum* 'Beacon Silver' is one of the best.

Lonicera pileata: Low-growing evergreen ground cover with arching, horizontal branches. Good in sun or shade, with bright green spring foliage. Small, white flowers in spring are followed by unusual translucent violet berries.

Nepeta: Catmint or catnip, is one of the most useful ground covers in full sun and well-drained soils. I like to grow it under roses, which the purists consider sacrilege, but which looks great.

Pachysandra terminalis: Evergreen, suitable for deep shade, with white flowers. Relatively slow to establish, it enjoys acid soil. There is also a useful variegated form.

Polygonatum: Solomon's seal is excellent in shade and in deep, rich, damp soils. The greenish-white bell-shaped flowers appear in late spring.

Pulmonaria: *P. saccharata* is the lungwort most commonly grown, and it does well in full or partial shade, preferring a moist but not waterlogged soil. Attractively blotchy leaves, and pink and blue flowers in spring.

Stachys byzantina: Lamb's lugs or lamb's ears, with their soft, felty grey leaves, are excellent in full sun and poor soils. The cultivar 'Silver Carpet' is especially good as ground cover.

Symphoricarpos x *chenaultii* 'Hancock': Provides good ground cover for both sun and shade, even when planted beneath trees. The white flowers are insignificant, but the whitish pink berries that appear in autumn continue well into winter.

Symphytum grandiflorum: Good, spreading ground cover beneath trees in moist, cool soil. Flowers for a long period in spring, with creamy tube-like flowers.

Vinca minor: The periwinkle is an invasive evergreen, happy in sun or shade, with blue flowers borne over a long period. There is a variegated form, and a variety with larger flowers, *V. major.*

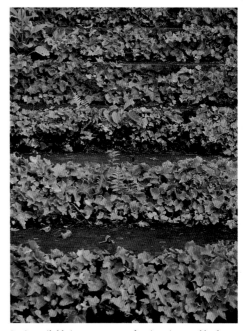

Ivy is available in a vast range of variegations and leaf shapes. I favour the simpler green varieties – the risers of these steps are transformed by such planting.

This is the perfect marriage of hard and soft landscaping, the slabs forming an abstract chequerboard pattern that is softened by the luxuriant carpet of moss. A rampant ground cover such as this should either be contained or, if space permits, allowed to drift off into an informal area where it can fade out without being too invasive.

While any garden will have finite boundaries, it may also have internal divisions, enclosing different areas.

Boundaries

The prime object of a boundary is to enclose the garden. But it can also provide privacy, afford shelter from wind or noise, and keep people or animals inside or out.

Where privacy and shelter are important a solid boundary of some kind – possibly reinforced with planting to act as an additional filter for the wind – is probably the best option. A country garden with fine views might be better served by an open post-and-rail fence, or sunken ha-ha.

Boundaries, as paving, can extend the visual line of a house to incorporate the wider setting. A brick or stone wall would make a natural continuation from a building of the same material, which will in turn help to create a link between the often disparate entities of house, garden and surrounding area.

Hard boundaries may be built from more than one material: a brick wall with panels of broken flint, or well-detailed stone piers with trellis or panel inserts can look superb. In general, however, they are most sucessful when you keep the design simple and respect local traditions.

Cost, of course, is also an important factor and as a boundary may well consume a substantial part of your budget, it makes sense to weigh up the alternatives with care. Walls are expensive, post-and-wire fences far cheaper, but cost should be considered in relation to the job they need to do.

For many of us, a fence is the most practical and cost-effective solution, and this will often take the form of timber panels or boards. Hedges can be cheaper yet equally effective; they make excellent windbreaks and are a good backdrop for planting – although obviously they take time to establish.

Opposite: Boundaries frame a garden. They can be blended and hidden or make a statement. Here, the smooth rendered concrete stands out against the dramatic foliage above.

It is important to consider gates and entrances when you are thinking about your boundary, but it is surprising how often they are simply slotted in with no real thought. The only absolute rule when you design a gate is that it should be in harmony with the rest of the fence, wall or divider.

Screens and Dividers

A garden that can be seen in a single glance is usually far less interesting than one that is divided into separate rooms, each with its own character.

Well-positioned dividers create a feeling of mystery, tension and surprise. We never fail to be attracted by the mystery of what lies beyond a wing of trellis, a hedge or, on a larger scale, a well-planted avenue. As we approach, there is a feeling of anticipation which is released only by the delight of discovery as the new space is entered.

Like most of the designer's 'tricks of the trade', the choice of materials to divide a space depends on familiar criteria: the style of the surrounding garden, common sense, an appreciation of scale, the use of form and, of course, sensible positioning!

Above: *Dividers not only separate different areas of the garden but also contain individual spaces. Where a screen is pierced, plants can be allowed to grow through: here the fence rises through green clouds of* Alchemilla mollis.

Below: *Boundary treatments are infinitely variable and this juxtaposition of solid piers and light timber rails is a fascinating contrast in materials and form.*

DRY-STONE WALLS

This dramatic and beautiful dry-stone wall uses a wide range of materials to form a composition that is more a work of art than a standard boundary treatment. The planting at a higher level provides an effective counterpoint to the delicate stonework.

BUILDING A DRY-STONE WALL

Set a dry-stone wall over a foundation of large stones before building the wall to a taper or 'batter' which will help to provide extra stability.

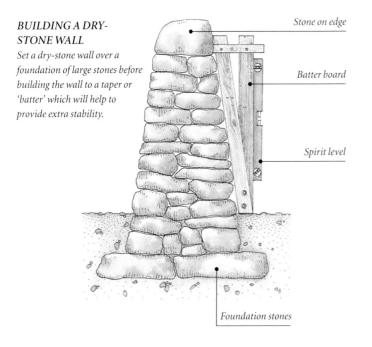

Stone on edge

Batter board

Spirit level

Foundation stones

Characteristics: Dry-stone walls were originally used as field boundaries, and have a strongly regional and rural character. This makes them look totally comfortable in an area where such stone is found naturally, and outrageously pretentious elsewhere. They are commonly found in many parts of the British Isles, and in rural areas throughout the world.

The quality and colour of stone varies enormously: grit, limestone, sandstone, granite and slate may all show subtle variations within the space of a few miles. The character of the walls is also affected by the natural irregularity of the stones, which are often simply gathered from the surrounding land. Even when perfectly laid, the faces will have rich textures and shadows, and pockets of soil will allow sprawling plants to be introduced, reinforcing the informal effect. Flatter, less rounded stones are normally selected as these provide the greatest stability. Because no mortar is used, dry-stone walls should never be built to more than waist height, and while this will provide a physical boundary, it will not ensure privacy.

Uses: Dry-stone walls translate happily into a village environment, but look distinctly out of place in the more formal character of a town. They look perfectly at home surrounding a field or a large country garden. They also look comfortable framing a much smaller space where the house, too, is built of stone, and will provide a natural link between the two. They should not be used for load-bearing or for more substantial constructions, but are excellent for raised beds, dividers and for low retaining walls too.

Construction: This is a skilled job, best undertaken by local craftsmen, with much of the skill lying in the selection of stones during construction. Foundations are usually minimal and simply consist of large slabs of stone laid well beneath ground level. The wall is built in two halves, with the centre packed with rubble. Larger stones are used at the bottom, and smaller at the top, to ensure that both faces are angled slightly inward towards the top. Some craftsmen use a spirit- or carpenters' level placed against a special wooden template to ensure that this 'batter' is correctly aligned.

Walls can be regularly or randomly coursed, depending very much on the shape of the stone, and are reinforced by the addition of through stones running from one side to the other, as work progresses. Gaps between stones are wedged with slivers of rock. Coping often takes the form of stones set on edge; where these are alternately higher or lower, they are known as 'cocks and hens'.

Dry-stone walls should always follow the lie of the land, and should never be stepped up or down.

Contrasting & associating materials: Dry-stone walling associates naturally with gravel and stone paving. It also looks particularly handsome with timber: well-detailed fencing, railway sleepers or decking. Siting decking close to dry-stone walling can look effective when used in a contemporary cottage garden.

This wall displays craftsmanship at its very best, and has been built in courses using carefully selected stones of roughly similar thickness but different lengths. Additional character, colour and texture are provided by the lichens that have colonized the wall face.

STONE HEDGES & TURF BANKS

Stone banks have a deliciously rural feel, and will only look comfortable if they are constructed in an area with appropriate surroundings. Plants will readily colonize, but you can give them a helping hand by scooping out pockets and introducing material artificially.

Characteristics: Stone hedges and turf banks are strongly regional, rural boundary treatments that look best in their own locality. They are predominantly found in the west of England and in certain other parts of the world. Both have a core of rammed soil, so the overall width is relatively great, and they are rarely built over chest height.

Uses: Both can be used to provide a subtle link between garden and landscape, with plants introduced, or allowed to self-seed, on their face. They are totally stock-proof and can make a superb boundary for a large country garden adjoining farmland or paddocks, but their bulk makes them unsuitable for small spaces.

Construction: Skilled and practised craftsmen are essential, and it is a sad fact that these folk are becoming harder to find. Both stone hedges and turf banks are built with a pronounced batter, and turf banks especially are considerably wider at the bottom than the top. Stone banks are built in a similar way to dry-stone walls, but with soil used between the stones. The core in each case is made from a mixture of stone and rammed soil, the soil usually being taken from one side to form a ditch. Turf banks are then covered with sods held in position with wooden pegs until they take hold, and stone hedges are faced with stones of varying size.

Contrasting & associating materials: Such a strong feature needs a strong use of materials around it. Natural stone paving, gravel, chippings and timber in the form of railway sleepers or logs all associate well.

MORTARED STONE WALLS

Mortared stone walls can last a very long time and often provide an ideal host to all kinds of planting. This example shows a particularly good method of dealing with a gateway: the line of the wall has been gently swept over the top of the gate in a rhythmical curve.

Characteristics: A well-built and carefully pointed mortared stone wall will have the same characteristics as a dry-stone wall, and like it, will look best in regions where stone occurs naturally. Aesthetic considerations will be the same. The difference is that a mortared wall is considerably stronger and can therefore be built to a greater height.

Uses: Since mortared stone walls can be built to about 1.8m (6ft) in height, they can be used where privacy is important. They can also be used for load-bearing, or as retaining walls – either on their own or as facing for brick or concrete blocks.

Construction: Unlike dry-stone walls, mortared stone walls can be built by any competent bricklayer. Methods vary in different areas, and it is important to look around for good examples, and appreciate the skills involved. Concrete footings should suit the ground conditions, and be about twice as wide as the 450mm (18in) base of the wall. Like a dry-stone wall, the mortared wall is built in two halves, with a core of rubble running through the centre, but usually without through stones. It can either be built to a batter, or vertical, and will look best if it is coursed. Courses can be made up of different-sized stones: one course of 70mm (3in) stones, one of 150mm (6in) stones, a third of 100mm (4in) stones, for example. Occasional jumpers (larger stones that span two courses) can be inserted as work progresses.

Careful pointing is essential. This can either be raked back to create shadows that will emphasize the strongly textured face, or neatly rubbed to provide a softer, indented joint. Mortar that is squashed out of the joints like toothpaste simply degrades the stone.

Coping can be the traditional stone on edge, a rounded fillet of mortar, or even brick on edge. My own house is built of pale Northampton stone, and I have constructed walls of the same material. The coping consists of a double row of blue bull-nosed engineering brick, which matches the slate roof of the house and contrasts beautifully with the stone.

Contrasting & associating materials: Natural stone paving, gravel or chippings. Solid timberwork such as railway sleepers or decking. Sections of slatted timber fence can also look handsome if the overall run is carefully integrated.

BUILDING A MORTARED STONE WALL
Like unmortared walls, these gain added strength if they are built to a batter. Use raked or rubbed back joints for the pointing.

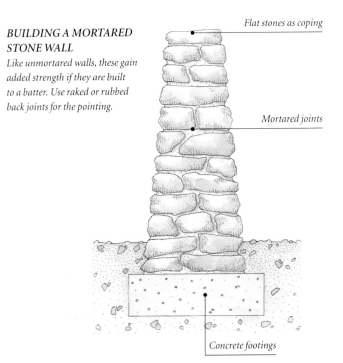

Flat stones as coping

Mortared joints

Concrete footings

STONE BLOCKS

HA-HAS

This generous arch has enormous visual power and is built from large pieces of dressed stone, softened by the overhanging fronds of ivy. The theme is continued at ground level where the stonework of the arch is reflected in the intricately worked pattern of setts.

New ha-has are expensive to build but, in the right setting, they can be well worth their high cost. Attention to detail is always important, and the vernacular construction of brick and flint in this contemporary example matches the materials used in the nearby house.

Characteristics: Sawn, or dressed, stone is the king of walling, but this beautiful material is so expensive that it is only really viable for very high-cost projects. Like all natural stone, it has enormous colour and textural variations, depending on its source, and the smooth face will also be dressed with different textures; pouncing (an indented finish) is popular in certain parts of the country. Blocks are usually regular in size, which helps to create a crisp, architectural pattern. Joints are pointed with mortar to match the stone; these are either left flush, or carefully raked back to provide well-defined shadow lines.

Uses: Walls made of sawn stone are traditionally used for fine houses and adjoining boundaries in both town and country, but they can be used to devastating effect with both traditional and contemporary architecture. They are perfect in areas where the stone is quarried. In a garden setting, stone can be used as a frame and teamed with brick. Stone walls topped with wrought-iron railings are exceptionally elegant, though horrendously expensive.

Construction: This is firmly in the realm of the stonemason; if you can afford the stone, you can also afford the professionals to put it up! Solid concrete foundations are essential, and the mortar should contain stone dust so that it matches exactly. Coping is usually made from natural stone, often carefully shaped to a traditional profile.

Contrasting & associating materials: Stone walls and gravel drives are quite simply close to God. They look good, too. Elegant planting schemes of hardy perennials, sweeping English lawns and a carefully parked Aston Martin DB5 complete the picture – dream on!

Characteristics: Ha-has were one of the great landscape devices of the eighteenth century. They consisted of a sunken ditch, faced on the house side with a retaining wall and often with a fence at the bottom, that allowed a view to run smoothly out into the surrounding parkland, while preventing cattle or other livestock from getting in. The object was to provide an apparently seamless transition from the grass in front of the house into the landscape beyond, and the spoil from the ditch was often used to create a smooth ramp up to the ha-ha from the house, which augmented the effect still further.

Uses: Ha-has are still built today, and if the budget will stand the cost, make a far better boundary than the over-used and obtrusive post-and-rail fence. The line of the ha-ha can be continued with a fence, once the boundary is hidden from the house or main viewpoint.

Construction: Ha-has require a great deal of excavation. In a parkland setting, the distance from one end to the other may be considerable, and the ditch itself will be at least 1.8m (6ft) deep, with a retaining wall of the same height. The wall may be built of concrete blocks but is usually faced in brick, brick and flint, or stone, depending on the local material, and angled into the bank to form a slight batter. The installation of land drains may be necessary to prevent the ditch becoming a moat.

Contrasting & associating materials: Not applicable.

BRICK WALLS

Characteristics: One of the oldest constructional materials known to man, brick is produced today in much the same way as it was thousands of years ago. It confirms the old adage that the simplest things work best: bricks are simply rectangular blocks of burnt clay; easy to make, easy to lay, and exceptionally durable. Brick is also beautiful, showing huge variations in colour and texture – variations that depend on the local clay and the length of firing time in the kiln. If you cross any country that produces brick, you will notice these local variations, especially in the vernacular architecture; it was not so long ago that every town and village had its own brickworks, producing bricks that looked comfortably at home in the built environment.

The same is true of garden walls. You will see both fine old walls and new ones that extend the line and character of a building into the wider landscape or townscape. They provide a cue to the use of a similar brick within the garden, either as dividers or floors.

This is a perfect example of hard landscape at its best. Old brick has a mellow character that can often compensate for slight irregularities in construction. The steps, with tile risers that match the colour of the brick, and punctuated by delicate star-like daisies, effectively extend the line of the wall out into the garden.

DOUBLE THICKNESS BRICK WALL

Always build foundations to twice the width of the wall and deep enough to suit your soil conditions. Insert pegs at regular intervals and to the same height, then bring the concrete up to the tops of the pegs. Flemish bond has been used here, with a radiused brick coping.

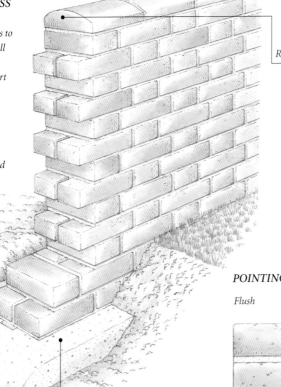

Radiused brick coping

Level pegs for foundation

Concrete foundation

CONCRETE COPING WITH DRIP CHANNELS

Coping prevents dampness percolating down from the top of the wall.

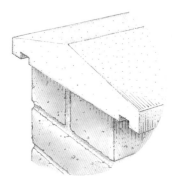

POINTING STYLES

Flush

Weathered

Rubbed back

Pointing prevents dampness penetrating the joints of a wall. The style of pointing chosen will considerably alter the look of a wall.

This unusual screen wall uses bricks in a design based on diagonals. The coping is complex, using specially moulded bricks and provides visual stability to the top of the run,

while the vine softens the outline and frames the simple timber seat. Such a wall forms a practical screen, yet allows tantalizing glimpses of the surrounding garden.

Uses: As brick is a small module and easy to lay, its uses are almost limitless. Boundary walls are an obvious choice, but so, too, are screens and internal divisions, retaining walls, raised beds, water features, barbecues, steps, garden buildings, pillars to support pergolas, overheads and arbours, and many other features. Used as a boundary it will ensure continuity; used as an accent it provides punctuation. Brick walls can be straight or curved, staggered or interlocking. They form a superb backdrop to planting, and if facing the sun, will hold the heat to provide an added bonus for growing conditions. A pierced honeycomb wall will provide a delightful screen as well as making an effective windbreak, and because of the flexibility of the material, is as easy to construct as an arch. Brick can also be used as a frame for other, more random materials, such as broken flint or stone.

Construction: All brick walls need sound foundations, or footings, twice as wide as the finished wall, and sufficiently deep to provide stability in the prevailing ground conditions. Footings should always be below the level of surrounding topsoil, and be taken down into undisturbed ground.

As a general rule, a wall that is built using a double layer of bricks both looks, and is, far stronger than a single thickness brick wall. The cost will be higher, but as a wall can stand for many hundreds of years, the initial outlay is well worthwhile. The pattern of bricks used in a wall is called the bond, and different bonds produce very different effects. These bonds give the wall its inherent strength, and the patterns are formed from stretchers (bricks laid along the face of the wall) and headers (bricks laid through the wall). It is unfortunately the case that bricklayers often

use Flemish bond today, rather than English or English walling bond, both of which are visually rather more interesting.

Curved walls are inherently stronger than a straight run, and a staggered wall, with one right-angle butting into another, will be both strong and provide interesting bays and angles as a backdrop for planting. A long run will be subject to slight expansion and contraction in different temperatures, and it is prudent to incorporate expansion joints every 10–12m (32–40ft). In effect, this means that you will have a series of walls, separated by a gap about the width of your finger which will be filled either with a treated board or mastic.

Pointing, which keeps the weather out of the face of the bricks, has great visual impact, and should always be carried out neatly. Joints can be 'weathered' at an angle, 'rubbed back' to form a U-shaped joint, or 'raked out' to form a crisp shadow line that will emphasize the individual modules. When carrying out renovations, any new pointing should match the old.

While you probably will not need to worry about rising damp in garden walls, a suitable coping is necessary to keep the weather out of the top. By far the best coping for a brick wall is bricks laid on edge; this is simple, unpretentious, and does the job in hand. Occasionally you will see stone coping on brick walls. This can look superb but, unfortunately, it tends to cost a fortune. Well-made pre-cast concrete coping is perfectly acceptable, but virtually anything else that may be suggested by your trendy architect should be avoided like the plague!

Contrasting & associating materials: Brick is the cosmopolitan of the landscape world, forming a superb background, or blending in with the widest possible range of other garden materials. There is a brick for every situation, whether it be a crisp, shiny engineering brick, or a rustic stock. The secret of success, as with everything else in the garden, is good design, with a lack of ostentation and over-complication.

CONCRETE BLOCKS

The simple approach so often works best; these concrete blocks, laid to form a honeycomb wall, blend perfectly with the gate piers and the adjoining building. The gates themselves are great fun, the colour picking up that of the shutters.

Characteristics: Concrete blocks provide an eminently sensible and low-cost material for all types of walling. Blocks measure either 225 x 225 x 450mm (9 x 9 x 18in) or 100 x 225 x 450mm (4 x 9 x 18in), the large size being the stronger, and have either a slightly rough or a smooth face. Blocks can either be rendered, painted or, if constructed from an attractive aggregate, simply left as they are. Where new houses are built of the same material , concrete block boundary walls provide an ideal link between house and garden.

Uses: For freestanding and retaining walls and structures of all kinds. Their cheapness makes them especially suitable for a wide range of uses in utility areas of the garden. Laid with wide open joints they can be used to form a visually powerful 'honeycomb' wall. Their strength allows them to be used for high walls.

Construction: Sound foundations are essential, and should be twice as wide as the finished wall. Thinner blocks should only be used for fairly low walls, unless they are buttressed at regular intervals to give them additional strength. A simple stretcher bond is suitable for most walls. The best coping for a 225mm (9in) wall is brick laid on edge, while pre-cast concrete coping is most suitable for a 100mm (4in) wall. Pointing can either be flush, rubbed back or raked out. Alternatively, the surface can be painted or rendered.

Contrasting & associating materials: Concrete blocks usually look best in a contemporary setting, positioned alongside a house built in similar blocks or with rendered walls. Pre-cast concrete paving, *in-situ* concrete, gravel and timber in the form of decking or railway sleepers are all compatible.

RENDERED CONCRETE

Characteristics: In Britain, but fortunately not in other parts of the world, concrete is considered a cheap and nasty material. Cheap it may be (which is in its favour); nasty it certainly is not.

Rendered concrete walls form one of the most durable and cost-effective boundaries or dividers available. Built with a low-cost core of brick or concrete blocks, they can be finished in a wide range of renders: textured, patterned, pebble-dashed with small stones just after the wet mix has been applied, or smooth – when it presents an ideal surface for painting. They are thus extremely adaptable, and can be blended into many different architectural and garden situations.

Uses: Rendered walls are the workhorse of many a garden, and are especially useful in a contemporary situation where adjoining buildings are also built of concrete. By using a colour wash, you can extend a colour scheme from inside to out, and produce an effect that is refreshingly clean and crisp. Such walls will also be an excellent low-cost choice for screening utility work areas or for use as retaining walls.

Construction: Sound foundations are needed, and should be twice as wide as the finished wall. The core should be built of brick or concrete blocks, and rendered to provide the final finish. A good coping is essential to keep the weather out of the top of the wall and prevent it loosening the render. Brick on edge is the best, but neat pre-cast concrete is also suitable.

Contrasting & associating materials: Rendered walls often look best in conjunction with contemporary materials such as pre-cast concrete paving, brushed aggregates, decking, and chunky timbers, such as railway sleepers. They also associate well with crisp, well-detailed timber fences.

Do not be afraid to use strong tones. The warmth of this colour-washed and crudely rendered wall brightens up this courtyard and blends well with the terracotta tiles of the floor. Such a confident treatment will almost certainly reflect the character of the owner.

If you have the right setting, concrete can be one of the most visually organic materials at your disposal. This wall and gateway has an enormous feeling of strength and movement.

Rendering a surface not only softens the outline but can be used to create many other varied effects, some of which may reflect a strongly regional flavour.

IN SITU CONCRETE

Characteristics: Go to any American town or city, and you will see *in situ* concrete used in the most imaginative and elegant ways. It is immensely strong – truly the stone of the twentieth century. Because the walls require some kind of casing or shuttering to hold the wet concrete in place until it hardens, an infinite variety of finishes is possible. Heavily grained boards can be used to impart their pattern to the finished wall, and the boards themselves can be of varying widths and set at different depths to set up fascinating rhythms on the exposed surface. Alternatively, the surface can be mechanically hammered to create ribbed and indented patterns of all kinds. Runs need not be straight; curved concrete walls are easily built, which opens up all kinds of exciting design possibilities. The only important thing is to make sure that the wall is in keeping with its surroundings.

Uses: In situ concrete walls can be used in the widest possible range of situations. Although normally used in contemporary designs, they can, if great design skill is exercised, be used to superb effect alongside traditional materials or in historic settings. Walls like these can form an obvious extension to a house built of similar materials, and would be an excellent choice for retaining walls and other load-bearing structures.

Construction: These walls are cast in their entirety, including the foundations below ground level, and steel reinforcing rods are often used to give internal strength. Walls can be either vertical or battered (tapered), and shuttering will be required to hold the wet concrete in place. This is usually timber – either boards or large sheets of plywood – and must in turn be held in place by a framework of timbers. The concrete must be thoroughly compacted often with a mechanical vibrator, throughout the pouring process, and the shuttering must not be struck (removed) until the wall has hardened completely.

Contrasting & associating materials: Being so versatile, *in situ* concrete works well with virtually anything around it. The critical factor is the sympathetic design of the wall.

There are certain situations in which gardens, or parts of gardens, can be left completely free of plants. This is a stunningly simple and powerful use of concrete, as well as being a study in colour, form, texture and shape.

This is a restrained, low-maintenance composition with a Japanese influence. The utter simplicity of the smooth concrete walling, impeccably fitted around the old tree, provides the perfect link with the adjoining house.

48

ALTERNATIVE MATERIALS

This is pure abstract art, using a variety of different materials, patterns and colours to build up an overall picture that runs on either side of a heating duct. So often such a situation would be handled in a far less imaginative way.

Characteristics: Walls can be built from all kinds of materials in addition to the ones mentioned above. You only need to look around you to see the possibilities. The great architect Sir Edwin Lutyens, a master of the vernacular, employed a wide range of local materials to superb effect; these included slate and tiles used with intricate detailing to frame panels of brick or stone. Honeycomb walls, usually constructed from bricks with a gap left between each, can also be made from clay land drains, with one course stacked on top of the next and carefully mortared in position. Half-round ridge tiles can be used to create screen walls, or dividers, and create a far more handsome effect than the dire pressed concrete examples that I propose to ignore in this book. You can see superb examples of tile walls throughout the Mediterranean.

On a more contemporary note, glass blocks can be a lot of fun; they distort the image, allow light to filter through, and look fine in the right setting. I have myself used concrete lintels set vertically in the ground to form a fascinating screen, varying the height of the tops to set up terrific rhythms. The crucial thing is to use your imagination. I am waiting for a client bold enough to allow me to build a glass or acrylic wall filled with oil that is heated and lit from below. The effect at night would be simply stunning, with bubbles rising and falling in great amoebic shapes!

Uses: Alternative walls can be used almost anywhere. The prime rule is sensitive design and lateral thinking – as well as a sense of humour!

Construction: This will vary according to the materials chosen.

Contrasting & associating materials: Variable, contemporary or traditional. It is worth remembering that hi-tech materials can look brilliant in an historic setting. It is a shame that few people have the ability or the courage to experiment in this direction.

Glass blocks have been used here to form a light and attractive screen, the distortion being enough to prevent a direct view through the boundary. The main psychological problem that may need to be overcome here is the feeling that you are being looked at!

PANEL FENCES

Interwoven panels, and variations on the theme, can form an excellent and neutral boundary once they have weathered down. Ivy is a fine climber, particularly in shade, but needs to be prevented from forcing its way between slats and causing damage.

Characteristics: Panel fences are relatively cheap, easy to erect, and last for anything from ten to twenty years, provided they are properly maintained. Most are made from interwoven slats of thin timber, set within a frame and fixed between posts set firmly in the ground. The length of each panel is usually 1.8m (6ft), but the height can be anything from 900mm (3ft) to 1.8m (6ft).

Most panels are pre-treated with preservative, but the colour is often very pale, making them glaringly obvious. The secret is to tone them down with a darker preservative, allowing them to merge into the landscape and providing a better backdrop for planting. Panel fences should be unobtrusive, and not, like some other fences, used as a feature in their own right; their visual strength lies in their uniformity, providing a neutral background that does not shout for attention.

Uses: As boundaries, dividers, screens for utility areas, fencing for dog runs, and many other kinds of enclosure. Being solid, they can provide privacy, and they are strong enough to keep people or animals in or out.

Construction: Panels are fixed to posts that are either concreted into the ground or slotted into metal shoes. The tops of the posts should be capped and kept flush with the panels. Each panel, topped with a capping rail, should be fitted at about 150mm (6in) above ground level to minimize rotting – the gap may be bridged by replaceable gravel boards nailed between the posts. Apply an annual coat of non-toxic preservative (never creosote, which will damage plants) to both panels and posts.

Contrasting & associating materials: If stained the right colour, they will blend into a wide range of situations.

ERECTING A PANEL FENCE
Panels are widely available and they are easy to erect between posts to make one of the cheapest of fences.

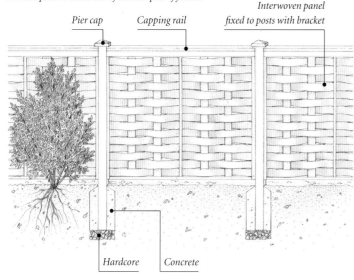

Pier cap   Capping rail   Interwoven panel fixed to posts with bracket

Hardcore   Concrete

CONCRETE SPUR
Attach concrete spurs to the bases of timber posts to prevent them from rotting. Gravel boards running between posts can easily be replaced if they start to decay.

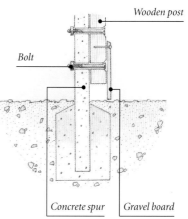

Wooden post

Bolt

Concrete spur   Gravel board

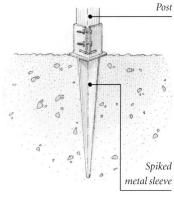

Post

Spiked metal sleeve

METAL POST SUPPORT
Metal spikes must be driven absolutely vertically into the ground. This task can be made simpler by using adjustable supports.

CLOSE-BOARD FENCES

This is an attractive and unusual variation on a close-board fence, where wide and narrow boards are set alternately, the latter bridging the gap and providing additional vertical emphasis. Such fences can be painted to blend with the house or another colour scheme.

CONSTRUCTING A CLOSE-BOARD FENCE
Close-board fences are more expensive than panels, but normally last longer and can conform to sloping or rolling ground.

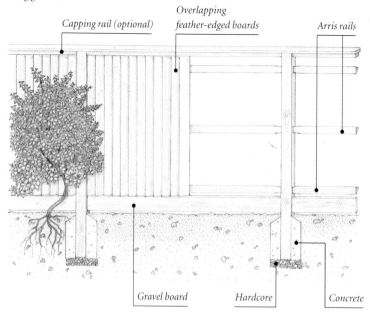

Capping rail (optional)

Overlapping feather-edged boards

Arris rails

Gravel board   Hardcore   Concrete

Characteristics: Close-board fences belong to the large family of fences in which individual slats or boards are nailed vertically to horizontal rails set between posts. They are strong, durable, unobtrusive, provide privacy, and form excellent secure boundaries. They are usually 1.8m (6ft) high, but may be more. They are more complicated to erect than panel fences, the work usually being carried out by specialist contractors, and the cost is therefore correspondingly greater. As with any outdoor timber constructions, they should be treated regularly with a non-toxic preservative to prevent rot.

Uses: Primarily as medium-cost secure boundaries. close-board is particularly suited to sloping or undulating ground, where the fence can follow the contours of the land. Because boards are fitted individually, they can allow for a tree or other feature to protrude through the boundary fence – something that is impossible with a panel fence.

Construction: Posts must be fixed securely into the ground 1.8m (6ft) apart, set in concrete, with two or three horizontal arris rails slotted into mortices cut in the posts. The overlapping boards are usually 150mm (6in) wide and feather-edged, which means that the thickness tapers from one side to the other. The top of the run is not normally capped, but replaceable gravel boards are fitted at the bottom.

Contrasting & associating materials: Like panel fences, close-board fences are intended to provide an unobtrusive background, and should be stained to achieve this. They are particularly successful in a woodland setting, where the vertical line blends well with trees.

This close board fence has been fitted above a low wall of burnt bricks topped with a crisp engineering-brick coping. Such a treatment could easily have ended up as a muddle, but it works well, the strong colour drawing the gate and house into the composition.

SLATTED FENCES

slats create a feeling of space – a particularly useful design tool in a small garden. As well as varying the width of boards, you can also vary the height of the fence; this is especially pertinent for screens and dividers. Design permutations are many and various; boards can be set diagonally as well as horizontally or vertically, and here you can stamp your own individuality on your boundary or internal divider – provided you carry out your plans with sensitivity and respect for your neighbours.

Uses: Slatted fences are almost invariably used as a contemporary design element, and generally look their best in such situations. For inspiration, look around you at well-conceived housing developments, or at places where good garden designers or landscape architects have been at work.

This highly individualistic slatted fence has been specifically designed to fit a particular situation. The rhythm of the swooping cut-outs is echoed on a smaller scale by the balls on the tops of the posts.

CONSTRUCTING A SLATTED FENCE

It is possible to build slatted fences to the widest range of patterns, using boards of different widths. The direction of boards will provide visual emphasis.

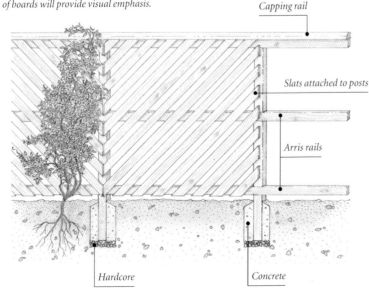

Capping rail

Slats attached to posts

Arris rails

Hardcore

Concrete

Characteristics: Vertically slatted fences use posts and arris rails, but instead of one board overlapping the next, there is usually a gap between each. Horizontally fitted boards are simply fitted to the posts without any intermediate support. Timber is normally sawn and planed, providing a crisp architectural finish which can either be painted, to pick up a colour scheme on the house, or stained.

Slats may be broad, narrow, or a subtle mixture of both. Wider boards will provide a greater degree of privacy, but it is worth remembering that wide boards are visually dominant and tend to draw a boundary in, while narrow, delicate

Construction: Much the same as for close board fences. The slats are nailed to arris rails fixed between posts, and here precision is of paramount importance: any misalignment of slats will look dreadful. It is also worth noting that the thinner each individual slat, the more prone the timber will be to movement and twisting – a strong argument in favour of using well-seasoned hardwood from a reliable and renewable source.

Contrasting & associating materials: Slatted fences associate well with most modern materials. But designer fences look best in well-designed gardens – take heed!

PICKET FENCES

This is a classic example of the picket fence that has come to epitomize the typical cottage garden with its simple line and undemonstrative nature. These pickets have been painted in traditional crisp white, and the posts have been screwed securely to the rails to prevent them from twisting out of their strict formation.

This is an unusual variation on a picket fence, with a Japanese theme. Such fences are common in the Far East, but have a strong vernacular character that can be difficult to handle out of context. The method of fixing posts to rails is an integral part of the design.

Characteristics: Picket fences provide well-loved boundaries for period or cottage front gardens or yards. Usually relatively low – about 1m (3ft) in height – and often painted white, they offer no privacy and little in the way of shelter; most dogs can jump straight over them. Tops can be cut square, pointed, or rounded, and are sometimes pierced with fancy slots – a fussy and unnecessary detail.

Uses: Really only as demarcation. They can be used to pick up the colour and style of the house, especially if this is of timber construction, and can look a good deal more lively if painted in one of the stronger primary colours rather than the ubiquitous white.

Construction: These are simple to build. Posts are set approximately 1.2m (4ft) apart, with pickets fixed to two horizontal rails. Pickets should be the same height as the posts, and should be kept just clear of the ground. The gaps should be slightly narrower than the pickets.

Contrasting & associating materials: The ideal setting for these fences has almost become a cliché: old brick paths, natural stone paving, gravel, and masses of herbaceous planting. I need say no more!

RANCH FENCES

Ranch fences need not necessarily be the crisp white-painted affairs so common in suburban areas. A variation on the theme can often be seen in a far more rural setting, as here, where the boards are left unpainted and simply nailed to the posts in a far less formal way.

Characteristics: Ranch fences use wide horizontal boards instead of vertical ones, but still with a slight gap between each. They are reminiscent of the architecture of the 1960s and 1970s, and provided this looks good, so do they. They also look fine adjoining contemporary buildings, and provide a strong visual plane that can extend the clean lines of the house out into the garden.

Boards can be nailed to one side of the posts, or set alternately behind and in front – a technique known as 'hit and miss'. Fences are normally 1.8m (6ft) high, or more; in front gardens and yards they may be lower. They are often painted white, but this needs regular attention if the fences are not to look slightly seedy.

Uses: Ranch fences generally look better when used as boundaries rather than as dividers, but can be useful as a utility screen to run at right angles to a boundary.

Construction: Posts are set 1.8m (6ft) apart, and boards are planed smooth and should run absolutely horizontally. If the ground slopes, the fence should be stepped in sections.

Contrasting & associating materials: These fences look best in contemporary situations and alongside contemporary materials. They associate particularly well with overhead beams, especially if they have been constructed from similar planks and painted the same colour.

SINGLE RAIL FENCES

An unusual but interesting example of a single-rail fence; such a design would need to be positioned in a garden where a similar style of timberwork provided an overall theme. This example is both the right height and strong enough to double as an occasional seat.

Characteristics: Sometimes known as trip rails, these fences are usually no more than 600mm (2ft) high, and are often lower. Rails can be constructed from square section timber set into a V-groove in the top of the posts, or from metal tubes threaded through the posts.

Uses: Usually used as demarcation for front gardens, to prevent parking; or at the back of the house in situations where there is no need for a solid boundary (which might interrupt a fine view), and where privacy is not important. They can be used in contemporary and traditional situations. You will often see excellent examples in public open spaces such as parks.

Construction: Posts are set 1.8m (6ft) apart. Where rails are set in a groove, a metal strip the same width as the post is tacked to one side of the post, taken over both the rail and the groove, and nailed to the post on either side. Where a metal rail runs through the post, the top of the post can simply be neatly rounded off. If the construction is entirely of timber then this is normally stained; where a metal rail is used, the latter can be painted, perhaps to pick up on a colour scheme elsewhere.

Contrasting & associating materials: A simple fence like this is very undemanding, and will blend with a wide range of contemporary and traditional settings and materials.

POST-&-RAIL FENCES

I cannot help thinking of Huckleberry Finn when I see this type of post-and-rail fence! This beautifully weathered example suits its situation perfectly, blending well both with the area and surrounding buildings. The poppies are something else!

POST-&-ROPE FENCES

This is an excellent example of how posts and ropes should be put together, using solid uprights and double swags of cable. There is little privacy afforded by such a boundary, but it provides a wonderful vehicle for climbing plants of all kinds.

Characteristics: The over-used fence of paddocks, with horses gazing over them, and of pretentious gardens that can boast of anything approaching a good view. Although relatively cheap and easy to erect, post-and-rail fences can be dreadfully obtrusive if used in the wrong surroundings. They should, if possible, be hidden in a fold in the ground, or, if the budget will allow, replaced by a ha-ha or iron park fence. If you must have them, leave them natural; painted white, they are even worse.

Uses: They are really only suitable for keeping large animals such as horses and cattle out of the garden. Even these will either jump them or force their way through if they are sufficiently determined. You will have to nail sheep wire between the posts if you wish to keep smaller animals out or children in.

Construction: Fences can be either two- or three-rail, and are usually about 1.2m (4ft) high. Rough-sawn posts should be set approximately 1.8m (6ft) apart, and the cleft rails set in mortices. Hardwoods are the most durable choice.

Contrasting & associating materials: The strongly rural flavour of these fences means that they should be used only in the country, alongside lawns, grassland or crops. If you plant next to them, animals will lean over and eat the lot.

Characteristics: Very occasionally you will see post-and-rope fencing used like single-rail fencing: low and as a demarcation. More often, it is used above eye level as a superb divider, and as a support for climbing roses and other climbers. Either one or two ropes can be used as swags; if a single rope is used, it must be a stout one or the feature will look flimsy.

Uses: This traditional garden feature, much loved by Gertrude Jekyll and her contemporaries, can be given a thoroughly modern treatment. I have occasionally used brightly coloured rope slung between equally bright poles! Although more often used as a divider, posts and ropes can also be run along the back of a border, used to flank a path, or to provide vertical emphasis around a focal point such as a circular pool or sunken garden.

Construction: Every aspect needs to be sturdy: posts should be at least 150mm (6in) square, and 1.8m (6ft) high and ropes at least 25mm (1in) thick. Ropes are threaded through holes in the posts, and it is essential to ensure that posts are the same distance apart, and that each loop is the same length.

Contrasting & associating materials: Usually best in a traditional setting, surrounded by complementary natural materials; occasionally effective in a hi-tech design, with synthetic and man-made items.

BAMBOO FENCES

This is the real thing, a proper Japanese garden with a superb bamboo screen, which encourages 'borrowed' landscape from the area beyond, and provides a strong physical boundary at the same time. The lashings are an integral part of the design.

Characteristics: These fences are traditionally found in the Far East where they are used in much the same way as reed in this country. You only need to visit Japan or study pictures of gardens in that part of the world to see what an elegant boundary the material makes.

Fences can be high, and closely woven from thin stems to provide privacy and shelter, or made as a much more open structure, using thicker stems to form a screen or open boundary.

Uses: Either as boundaries, or as screens or dividers within the garden. They do, however, have quite strong oriental connotations, so need careful handling if they are not to look rather ostentatious.

Construction: Closely woven fencing of this kind is usually available in panels, and can be carefully wired to stout bamboo posts driven into the ground. Screens are normally made up on site from lengths of bamboo cut to size and tied to posts. They are best, and traditionally, tied on to the posts with twine – which needs to conform to a set pattern to be technically correct.

Contrasting & associating materials: Solid bamboo fences have a simplicity of line that makes them look comfortable in many contemporary settings. They also make a superb backdrop for all kinds of planting. Bamboo screens will really only look correct in a garden that has strong Japanese overtones.

On this delightful roof garden, thin bamboo canes have been laced together to form panels and set behind a stout timber framework. Such fencing provides attractive, unobtrusive shelter and makes the perfect background for planting of all kinds.

WATTLE, OSIER & REED FENCES

Reed fences provide a simple, unobtrusive and practical background and are used here to form an architectural enclosure for a pretty little parterre. As the weave is delicate, the seat is thrown into sharp contrast, providing the major focal point in the composition.

Whether they are made from split or whole stems, woven wattle hurdles provide an unobtrusive background that makes an ideal foil to plants. Panels normally measure 1.8 x 1.8m (6 x 6ft) and will last for approximately ten years.

The texture of woven osiers is delicate and delightful, as is the colour, but their life is limited and they are only suitable for relatively short-term use. Shadows set up endless patterns on the textured surface, forming a perfect backdrop to a border.

Characteristics: Wattle hurdles and osier or reed fences are all hand-made from local materials. Wattle hurdles, made from woven hazel stems, were originally used to pen sheep, and measure about 1.8m (6ft) square. They can be used to make a superb rural boundary that will provide an unobtrusive backdrop for planting. Their life-expectancy is only about ten years, but this is normally sufficient for a border or a hedge to have reached maturity. Only a few skilled craftsmen produce them today, so they are relatively expensive.

Osier panels are much the same as wattles, but use willow stems which are thinner and therefore have a finer visual texture. Reed fences are traditionally made in fen or river lowland areas where reeds grow naturally, and are sometimes made

in situ. The reeds are usually sandwiched between timber rails.

Uses: Although these fences look most at home in the country, they can also be strongly effective in an urban situation and against contemporary architecture. They all provide a complete screen, making them ideal for boundaries.

Construction: Panels are simply wired to round posts driven well into the ground.

Contrasting & associating materials: Because of their natural appearance and subtle texture, all these fences look handsome in a wide range of situations and against an equally wide range of materials, both traditional and contemporary.

PARK FENCES

WROUGHT- & CAST-IRON FENCES

Wrought iron is infinitely variable, looking equally at home in town or country. This screen and hooped pergola allows planting to scramble gently over the structure and encroach on the adjoining garden in a deliciously informal manner.

The characteristic boundary of country house estates, park fences are the ultimate retainers of a fine view, and, when painted black, hardly distract from the landscape beyond. This example has been fitted with thinner wire for extra security.

Characteristics: Metal park fences are the forerunners of timber post and rail fences, are used in similar situations, and, if you can afford them, are a far better proposition. You can still see long runs in parkland or along the edges of estates. The steel elements (originally iron) are considerably thinner than timber, and consequently far less visually intrusive; painted black, they become almost invisible. Most fences are 1.2m (4ft) high and are relatively stock-proof, but higher ones are sometimes required to keep deer in or out and these may be curved inwards at the top.

Uses: This type of fencing is still being produced, and is the perfect answer to a fine view. Even set against the horizon, it will barely disrupt it. It can often be used more cheaply for short runs, perhaps where a garden drifts out into woodland between two wings of planting.

Construction: Uprights consisting of a steel strip splayed out at the bottom should be set in concrete below ground level to provide stability. Three or four horizontal rails, either round or formed of a lighter strip, are then threaded through the uprights; a greater number will be needed for higher deer fences.

Contrasting & associating materials: Such a fence will usually be set in grassland, or between informal wings of planting, where it will look perfect – almost completely unobtrusive.

Characteristics: Traditional wrought-iron fences are usually superb, principally because of the craftsmanship involved and the quality of the materials used. If you have such a fence or divider, cherish it and maintain it well; it is priceless. The highly skilled craft of metal-working, where strips are fashioned and joined together, is making something of a comeback, and it is possible to obtain fine new fencing today, but it is extremely expensive. The advantage of a contemporary metal screen will be its delicacy and visual lightness. If you find the right thing, and can afford it, go for it! Popular low-cost contemporary versions are unfortunately a travesty of the real thing, and nearly always look over-complicated and flimsy.

Cast iron was much loved by the Victorians, and many fine fences still remain, though many British examples were melted down for weapons during World War II. Unfortunately, it is brittle and, once broken, almost impossible to repair.

Uses: All are suitable for fences, railings and dividers, though in different situations. Metal railings can look superb in conjunction with, or on top of, a wall.

Construction: This is in the hands of craftsmen and, unless you own a foundry or a forge, is beyond the average person's capability. Fixing such fences must also be left to the specialist landscape designer.

Contrasting & associating materials: Metal fences like these usually associate best with traditional settings and natural materials. Modern designs can obviously work well in a contemporary situation.

CORRUGATED IRON FENCES

Historically, corrugated iron has had a bad name, which is a pity as the modern forms can be used as worthwhile boundaries. It can be cut on an angle to match a slope, and here the colour of the fence provides a powerful visual link with that of the boards on the house.

Characteristics: Corrugated iron has long been used as utility fencing, but variations on the theme have brought it thoroughly up to date.

Uses: Sheet metal can be bent to various patterns and shapes, which can set up fascinating surface shadows. Colour can be imparted during the manufacturing process or painted after erection to link with a colour scheme on the house or elsewhere in the garden.

Construction: Metal posts should be concreted into the ground, with the corrugated iron panels bolted between them.

Contrasting & associating materials: Best in a contemporary setting with crisp, man-made materials.

Cast iron, or more often today, cast alloy, forms an elegant boundary, albeit one that provides little privacy. With this type of fence, planting can be encouraged to soften the line, blending the boundary out into the wider garden or landscape.

POST-&-CHAIN FENCES

Post-and-chain fences provide a sophisticated and traditional fence outside many a period property, although they offer little in the way of privacy. The posts can be painted, as here, to provide an effective visual link with adjacent paintwork.

Characteristics: Another fine traditional fence, which uses low timber posts or stone bollards with interlinking wrought iron chains. These are usually found at the front of fine period houses or flanking driveways, and are used as demarcation. Look around you for inspiration. Garden centres that sell plastic versions should be liquidated!

Uses: This elegant divider has no security or practical value, although it can be useful for preventing inconsiderate parking.

Construction: Posts are usually only about 450mm (18in) high, concreted into the ground, and are fitted with iron hooks just below the top. Chains are traditionally made from spiked links, though you will see other versions. Stone posts or bollards are usually craftsman-made, but are now also being manufactured in reconstituted stone.

Contrasting & associating materials: At their best in traditional settings, near similar materials. Can look superb set in grass or stone paving.

CHAIN-LINK FENCES

Occasionally, one fence type can be used in conjunction with another: here chain link has been set behind old iron railings to provide an impassable screen. It is remarkable just how unobtrusive chain link can be when used in an appropriate setting.

Characteristics: An underrated fence, all too often considered only in terms of security. It is certainly almost unsurpassed for this purpose, but can also be used as a boundary that allows a view to run into the garden. The only satisfactory version is one with plastic-coated posts and wire, and if these are brown or black, rather than the ubiquitous green, the fence will become almost invisible in the landscape. Height can vary from relatively low (the useless dividers that are found so often on housing estates) to high, for high security.

Uses: As an unobtrusive boundary, best sited at some distance from the house. Perfect, too, around a tennis court (here, again, brown or black is better than green). It is particularly effective behind tall planting, or running into woodland, where the mesh becomes almost invisible. It can provide support for twining plants, which can hide the fence completely. It can also be used behind an open fence, providing security for pets and children, as well as plant support.

Construction: Chain-link fencing will be supplied with everything you need. Posts will need concreting into the ground, and straining posts are often set at the ends of runs, or where the run turns through a right angle, and are bolted into the uprights to provide added strength. The chain link is connected to the uprights with metal strips threaded through the mesh and then bolted to the posts.

Contrasting & associating materials: The secret with chain-link fencing is that it should be invisible. If it is blatantly obvious it becomes pretty difficult to associate it with anything other than a scrapyard.

SYNTHETICS & REPRODUCTION TIMBER

Characteristics: One of the reasons why most garden design is about fifty years behind every other art form is because of our stubborn resistance to using synthetics in the garden. Ignoring the existence of plastics, polyesters and man-made fibres, is a form of horticultural snobbery, and the problem is compounded by the fact that garden centres do not sell them, and most garden designers have no idea about how to use them. Not only is there nothing wrong with using these materials, there are enormous advantages. They come in all kinds of exciting colours and textures, as well as being virtually indestructible, and I have had a lot of fun, and some success, experimenting with them myself.

One of the best synthetic fencing materials is the woven polyester used for cricket sight screens. It is light, rot-proof and translucent (which means that there is no problem with a shaded border). It is clipped into lightweight alloy panels bolted to alloy uprights. Unfortunately, it is only available in white; primary colours would be more exciting.

Nurserymen have long used windbreaks of tough plastic webbing stretched between timber posts, and this, too, could have a use in the domestic garden as a neutral (and completely rot-proof) background. I have also used thin plastic poles, set close together, as dividers. These *are* available in bright colours, and you can vary the height of the tops, swooping them up or down. They also sway in the wind, setting up their own rhythm and sounds. If you think laterally you might invent something unusual. Experimenting is fun, too.

Recycling is in vogue – quite rightly so – and there is now reproduction timber on the market that ingeniously solves the problem of what to do with spent polystyrene. It looks almost identical to wood, is just as strong and, although being relatively expensive, will last considerably longer than many natural timbers, being virtually rot-proof. It is normally available in boards – of varying widths and thicknesses – and also comes in a wide range of colours, which makes it useful to designers working with an overall theme in mind.

Uses: Alternative materials such as these can be used for both fences and screens. Reproduction timber can replace natural timbers in virtually all their applications, including overheads, pergolas, fencing and specialist woodworking. Because of its relatively high cost, it is best suited to high-profile projects, and would not be an economic option for more mundane carpentry.

Construction: You may need to work this out as you go. As with any job in the garden, fixings need to be secure and long-lasting. Reproduction timber is slightly harder than most natural timbers, but the carpentry skills required are identical.

Contrasting & associating materials: Most of the suggestions above will look best in a contemporary design, alongside contemporary materials. Just as with conventional timber, reproduction timber can be used for the widest possible range of purposes and design situations.

Reproduction timber looks pretty much the same as the real thing, but it is far more durable and comes in a wide range of colours. These overheads and trellis are an excellent example of its versatility and stability.

METAL GATES

Characteristics: Metal is an expensive material, and suspiciously cheap metal gates, like cheap metal railings, are rarely worth the money – especially if set in a mediocre wall of reconstituted stone. There is nothing to beat a fine old wrought-iron gate, and these can be found in all sizes from a simple pedestrian version to something huge and elaborate set in a wall at the entrance to a country estate. The important thing is that it should be right for its purpose; it is easy to be ostentatious!

Virtually all metal gates allow you to see straight through them, which will enable you to appreciate a fine view (in either direction) but will provide no privacy.

Uses: Metal gates can be used for pedestrian or vehicle access in situations where privacy is not important and where they are intended to last. They have obvious uses in traditional settings, but some stunning designs are now being produced, in both wrought iron and steel, that will enhance contemporary settings. They are ideal for linking dividers within the garden framework, heightening tension as you move between the different areas, and preventing access where necessary (for children or pets) while maintaining a view.

Construction: Metal gates require the skills of a blacksmith, or foundry, whether they be working to existing patterns or with new one-off designs.

Contrasting & associating materials: Metal gates usually look best set in substantial brick or stone boundaries; these have the visual strength to carry the fine detailing successfully. The setting can be traditional or contemporary, with materials to match.

Wrought iron work at its best is simply superb, having a delicacy and lightness of line that is impossible to achieve with other materials. Here the entire composition is in harmony, railings and gate being designed as one.

HANGING A METAL GATE
Always check the clearance of the gate before concreting the post in position. If there is sloping ground this must be allowed for, otherwise the gate will scratch the surface every time it is opened.

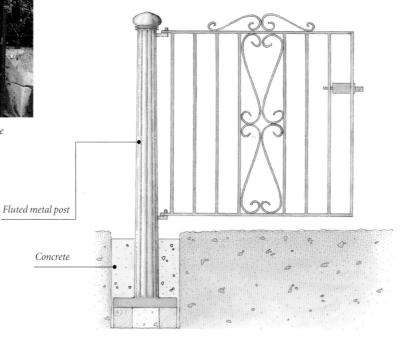

Fluted metal post

Concrete

There are places and situations you can simply dream about; in this setting all the various elements work beautifully together to form a stunning overall picture.

The juxtaposition of the boldly coloured vases and the delicately worked iron gates is pure magic; such is the stuff of outstanding design.

KISSING GATES

Metal kissing gates have a great feeling of delicacy and lightness, which is heightened when they are set within a boundary constructed from brick or stone, as here. Well-constructed examples will last almost indefinitely.

Characteristics: A charming and romantic way for pedestrians to pass through a boundary. The gate pivots within a framework, allowing one person to pass through at a time. If two attempt it, they get stuck – hence the name!

Normally waist-high, kissing gates are made either of timber or metal, and are usually designed to match the adjoining boundary. Both timber and metal kissing gates are found in low stone and brick walls.

Uses: As occasional gates into woodland or an adjoining field, or from one part of the garden to another. They are a prime example of a feature that affects the speed of movement through a space, and can be a useful design tool.

Construction: Timber is obviously easier to handle than metal, but both will need skilled workmanship. In both cases the design should be as unobtrusive and simple as possible.

Contrasting & associating materials: Metal kissing gates are purpose-made to match park fencing and, like the fencing, will look good with traditional and natural materials. Wooden gates blend most readily with fencing of the same material. Contemporary gates, made to crisp patterns and painted, look fine with similarly modern materials.

MOON GATES

This is an unusual moon gate in that it provides access through the boundary. There is a telling contrast between the solidity of the old brick wall and the much more delicate gate and railings. The view is an attractive one, drawing you into the next garden room.

Characteristics: These are not gates as such, but holes – usually circular – pierced in garden boundaries or dividers to embrace a view, an old landscape design device, which originated in the Far East. Moon gates need preceision positioning; they are not features to be overdone!

Moon gates can be set in brick, stone, or even well-designed fencing. The hole is usually left open, but attractive wooden shutters can be incorporated for security, privacy or shelter. Metal grilles can also be used, though these will not provide privacy or a windbreak.

Uses: As a landscape device, moon gates have great aesthetic value in the right setting, and a good view is of course essential. They are sometimes used, with mirrors positioned behind them, as a visual trick in small town gardens; this may be a clever idea, but it tends to smack of affectation.

Construction: Moon gates need to be substantial to be effective, and usually have a diameter of 1.8m (6ft) or more. The circumference of the circle should be finished in the same coping as that used for the boundary. If introduced into a timber fence the opening will need to be carefully cut out. Like the boundary itself, moon gates will probably require the skills of either a specialist bricklayer or stonemason. Wooden shutters can be quite straightforward to make; metal ones will require an expert.

Contrasting & associating materials: This will depend on the setting. Moon gates can be designed to suit both traditional and more contemporary gardens.

WOODEN GATES

A sense of fun is an invaluable part of good garden design, and this charming rustic gate is full of character. The colour combination is subtle and there is an initiative test incorporated in the design – how to undo the rope at the base!

Characteristics: The majority of boundaries are made from timber, and gates follow suit. As in all areas of design, simple solutions almost always work best: a straightforward ledge and brace design looks fine in a close board fence; a solid door looks best in a brick wall; and a picket-style gate suits a fence of a similar kind. Both hard and soft woods are used; both must be treated regularly with non-toxic preservative, or painted.

Pedestrian gates are sometimes combined with those for vehicles, the smaller side gate opens for people, the other for vehicles. Timber gates of this kind are often of the five-bar variety, and, again, the design should be kept simple; there are some appalling designs available which are really elaborate, and expensive too!

Uses: Simple timber gates, being so adaptable as well as cost-effective, can be used in virtually any situation, whether traditional or contemporary.

Construction: The simplest designs can be tackled by most people with basic carpentry skills and the right tools. More complex designs may require more sophisticated skills.

Contrasting & associating materials: There is really no limit to where or the materials alongside which such gates can be used; it is simply open to good design sense and imagination.

Some gardens and boundaries are simple and easy-going, and this delightful picket gate reinforces the relaxed surroundings. The old brick path meanders towards the entrance and the latter allows the view to drift through and above the boundary.

TRELLIS

Often, the simplest things work best of all in a garden: this straightforward squared trellis acts both as a divider between different areas of the composition and as a practical and attractive support for climbing plants.

CONSTRUCTING A TRELLIS DIVIDER
Trellis is available in panels of varying heights which can be fixed between posts.

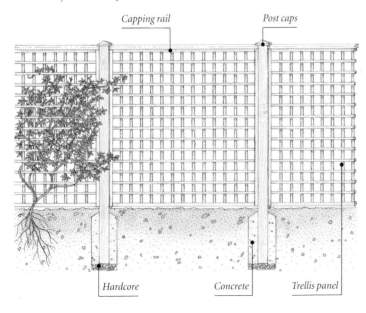

Capping rail
Post caps
Hardcore
Concrete
Trellis panel

Characteristics: Trellis is essentially an open structure, usually of timber though occasionally of metal, that allows the view to run through it whilst providing an ideal host for climbing plants. It comes in a variety of patterns, most of which are based on a diamond, rectangle, or square; you can even find one pattern of slats laid upon another, but a simple squared matrix probably forms the best background for plants. Lighter or heavier effects are achieved by the use of thinner or thicker slats in proportion to the gaps in between, and sturdier hardwood trellis (traditionally chestnut) is used for garden buildings. Standard panels are available from garden centres, and are usually 1.8m (6ft) square, but you can also get variations to fit specific situations, and tops may be scalloped or swept up into arched shapes of various kinds. Trellis is either painted or stained with preservative. Metal trellis is unusual, but you will find thick plastic-coated wire that looks flimsy, even though it is strong.

Uses: Trellis is one of the best dividers at the garden designer's disposal, and its delicacy makes it ideal for extending the line of a boundary unobtrusively into the garden. Wings of trellis, fronted by planting, are part of the essence of a traditional English country garden, and have the advantage of casting little shade.

Trellis can be used to raise the height of a boundary, and is often used on top of relatively low walls to improve privacy. It can also be used as panels on walls to support climbing plants, although horizontal wires are usually a better and more practical choice, and instead of low hedging to frame beds. In the more mundane parts of the garden, trellis can be used to screen utility areas or garden buildings. The fruit garden is an area in which trellis can be both practical and decorative, acting as a host for espaliers, cordons, vines and cane fruits. Such an area need not be simply a utility space, trellis can make it far more decorative, and draw it into the wider garden composition.

Construction: All too often, trellis panels look and are far too flimsy, and are made from untreated timber that is prone to rot. An ideal timber size for most trellis work is just under 20mm (¾in) square, while hardwood trellis looks better and will last for an exceptionally long time. Panels are fixed to posts, which are often supplied by the manufacturer in a specific pattern to match the trellis. They will need concreting into the ground or fitting with spiked metal shoes. The finished article may either be pre-painted by the supplier (an increasingly popular option) or stained with preservative.

Contrasting & associating materials: Trellis is an accommodating medium and fits comfortably into a wide range of situations, both urban and rural. The more contrived patterns need to be handled carefully, and blended into an appropriate garden style. Ready-stained trellis has become popular recently and can be obtained in a wide range of different shades. While this can justifiably link with adjoining colour schemes it is often used simply to be fashionable, which is *not* the best reason.

FEDGES

Fedges can play host to a wide range of plants, whether pelargoniums, as here, or species that lean against a surface, such as chaenomeles, climbers or annuals. The latter can either be contained in pots, hung on the frame or, if sufficiently rampant, trained from ground level.

CONSTRUCTING A FEDGE

This is a flexible feature and can be built to virtually any pattern. Sink hardwood posts approximately 450mm (18in) into the ground, before tacking on lengths of chicken wire or chain link fencing.

Characteristics: A fedge is a hybrid between a fence and a hedge. It comprises some kind of framework, over which a scrambling climber such as honeysuckle or ivy is grown. It looks like a hedge, but is far quicker to establish.

Uses: This device is ideal as a divider within a garden, and is usually best kept less than 1.5m (5ft) high, as taller than this climbers tend to become leggy and die out at the base.

Construction: The simplest frame consists of two rows of posts, approximately 600mm (2ft) apart in either direction, joined at the top by wires, and with wires running horizontally between them. Chicken wire or chain-link fencing is then stretched over the whole thing and tacked down firmly. Climbers planted on both sides are tied in as they grow, and quickly colonize the structure. Maintenance is limited to careful clipping or pruning.

Fedges are close relations of topiary, and ambitious practitioners can experiment with the final structural outline by modifying the underlying framework.

Contrasting & associating materials: Fedges will easily link with the overall style of the garden, whether this be traditional or contemporary, urban or rural, and, depending on the plant material used, can readily associate with hard or soft landscape materials.

FORMAL HEDGES

High drama is an integral part of many a fine garden, and this simple composition has immense power, generated by the high walls of beech that lead the eye down to the plain seat at the end of the vista. This is visual tension at its strongest.

Characteristics: Species that can be clipped to provide a crisp, unified appearance, such as yew and box, are obvious and traditional contenders for formal internal dividers and boundaries. The berries of yew are poisonous and this should be taken into consideration if there will be children in the garden or livestock in adjoining fields. Box or yew will make a stunning foil for pale planting, white seats and spring blossom. In a large garden, more textured beech, hornbeam, holly, privet, lonicera, even Leyland cypress can also be used as dividers, and form excellent boundary material.

Uses: Hedges are far more adaptable than fences or walls, and can be laid out, clipped, or allowed to grow, in any number of different shapes and patterns. The top of a boundary or screen can be crenellated or scalloped and wings can be made to swoop down to meet a path, heightening tension as you approach. Topiary ornaments can be introduced along their tops, and arches are easily formed. Cut-out 'windows' can, like moon gates, give glimpses of the room or the landscape beyond.

A crisp, textured, beech hedge could be used to provide a lively and windproof surround for an immaculate vegetable garden, or, brown in winter, as a subtle backdrop for the dark stems of a frosty orchard, or as a link with the thatched roof of a summerhouse. Low box hedging can be used to make an attractive frame to borders or pools.

Planting: The success of a hedge largely depends on thorough preparation of the ground before planting: a well-prepared trench, forked over at the bottom, and with a rich mixture of topsoil and well-rotted compost, is ideal. Hedging can be obtained 'bare rooted' for winter planting; root balled, also ideal in winter; or container grown, which is suitable for planting throughout the year. Hedges can be planted as a single or double row, the latter establishing an effective barrier rather quicker but needing more plants. Spacing will vary with the species chosen.

Correct clipping is vital. Formal hedges should be clipped to a slight batter, so that they are slightly wider at the bottom than the top. This will enable adequate light and moisture to reach all the branches, and will ensure that the hedge grows evenly.

CLIPPING A HEDGE

Clip hedges to a slight taper to allow light and air to reach all parts. This will ensure thick, even growth right down to ground level.

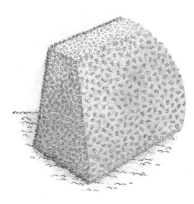

Contrasting & associating materials: Hedges are accommodating features, and do not set out to be stars in their own right. Formal hedging, however, associates especially well with crisp hard or soft landscape detail, and can look superb against sweeps of paving, gravel and manicured lawn.

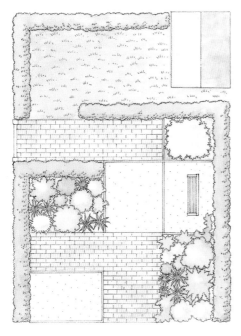

Do not be afraid of using rectangles. In this simplification of a modernist painting the hedging, planting and paving together build up a subtle pattern.

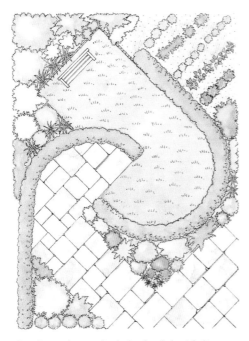

In a tiny garden, curving hedges break the sight lines, providing an air of mystery and surprise, as well as a feeling of space and movement.

Geometry is always an effective tool, and one of the garden designer's best allies. Planting hedges is often a far cheaper proposition than building expensive walls or dividers, and the solidity of this clipped box hedge creates a wonderful foil to the planting.

SUITABLE PLANTS FOR FORMAL HEDGES

HEDGING PLANT	PLANTING DISTANCES	CLIPPING REQUIREMENTS
Buxus sempervirens (box)	30cm (12in)	x 2–3 in growing season
Carpinus betulus (hornbeam)	60cm (24in)	x 1 mid- to late summer
Crataegus monogyna (hawthorn)	45cm (18in)	x 2 in summer/autumn
x Cupressocyparis leylandii (Leyland cypress)	75cm (30in)	x 2–3 in growing season
Fagus sylvatica (beech)	60cm (24in)	x 1 in late summer
Ilex aquifolium (holly)	45cm (18in)	x 1 in late summer
Ligustrum (privet)	30cm (12in)	x 2–3 in growing season
Lonicera nitida	30cm (12in)	x 2–3 in growing season
Taxus baccata (yew)	60cm (24in)	x 2–3 in summer/autumn
Thuja plicata (Western red cedar)	60cm (24in)	x 2 in spring/early autumn

INFORMAL HEDGES

Characteristics: Informal hedges can be used in many different situations, but are particularly suited to country gardens, where they can provide privacy and shelter, as well as a link with the surrounding countryside. The character of the garden will be determined as much by how tightly these hedges are clipped as by the species used. An enormous range of shrubs is available, some with the added bonus of flowers and/or fruit, and here imagination can be brought into play. As well as obvious choices such as hazel, hedges of *Escallonia*, shrub roses and forsythia can be used. Boundary hedges for country gardens are often mixed, including species such as hawthorn, field maple, hazel, elder, beech, dog rose, cherry, cornus, holly and wild viburnum. Some hedges are left unclipped and allowed to grow to their full height. Usually planted up with larger shrubs, they require space to accommodate the mature plants. Suitable species are often evergreen, have a dense habit, the bonus of flower, and height

Forsythia is a striking shrub, both in terms of its structure and its dazzling colour. Its springtime yellow will beckon, or possibly deter, any caller, and such a hedge is virtually impenetrable. *Such a vigorous hedge will need regular clipping and pruning to keep it under control, but where it is used as a positive statement it can be hard to beat.*

enough to provide privacy and shelter. A distant division of the garden, planted with a mixture of rosemary, *Lavatera* and *Cotinus coggygria* 'Royal Purple' is simply delicious.

Uses: Informal hedges make fine boundaries that will blend in with the landscape beyond, but most are just as comfortable in an urban setting. They can be used to separate different parts of the garden – the kitchen garden from a flower garden or lawn; the orchard from a field – and some, if properly laid, will provide an impenetrable barrier to keep stock out or in.

Because of their ultimate size, unclipped hedges are usually best sited well away from the house, and can be used to make a link with other planting in the area. They can look fine in the country, but are also useful in an urban or suburban setting, where there is space, and can even be used as dividers.

This is a multi-layered hedge, the background providing a physical barrier, with the hydrangeas in front giving extra visual interest and softening the line of the former. The lower hedge and edging plants in the foreground complete the composition, giving it real depth. Such a combination avoids the austerity of planting a single species.

Planting: As for formal hedging, thorough preparation of the ground is essential, and the same planting directions should be followed. Most hedges of this kind will need regular pruning if they are to be kept tidy, or more radical cutting back and layering every few years to keep them growing thickly and to prevent them from becoming leggy and too high. Even unclipped hedges may need some thinning or pruning, according to the species selected.

Contrasting & associating materials: It is important to choose the plant species to suit the setting, but most hedges will associate well with other materials. The more informal of these hedges are ideal for combining with rough grass, naturalized bulbs and wild flowers. An orchard bounded by sprawling dog roses is a delight.

Even a hedge that falls beneath eye level provides an effective divider, encouraging movement through space between different 'rooms' within the garden.

This is a delicious composition, with individual layers of different planting ranged formally in front of a delicate boundary of osiers. The planting embraces a number of different styles, with clipped lonicera giving way to a line of berberis and finally fastigiate conifers that echo the vertical line of the willow stems.

SUITABLE PLANTS FOR INFORMAL HEDGES

HEDGING PLANT	PLANTING DISTANCES	CLIPPING REQUIREMENTS
Berberis darwinii	45cm (18in)	x 1 after flowering
Corylus avellana (hazel)	60cm (24in)	x 1 after flowering
Escallonia	45cm (18in)	x 1 after flowering; remove old wood
Forsythia x *intermedia* (forsythia)	45cm (18in)	x 1 after flowering; remove old wood
Fuchsia magellanica (fuchsia)	45cm (18in)	x 1 in spring; remove old wood
Lavandula (lavender)	30cm (12in)	x 1 after flowering
Pyracantha	60cm (24in)	x 1 in spring; remove weak and vigorous stems
Shrub roses	45cm (18in)	x 1 in spring; remove weak stems

PARTERRES, KNOTS & MAZES

Characteristics: Scrolled *parterres de broderie*, ornamental knots and mazes have a long and distinguished history. Dating back many hundreds of years, they form important ingredients of many formal gardens.

Parterres and knots could be said to reflect the gardener's ultimate control of plant material, these intricate clipped patterns representing the dominion of mind over matter, as well as the sensitive manipulation of living material. Usually intended to be seen from above, their geometry never fails to catch the imagination. They were set pieces, intended for conversation and admiration, a far cry from the all-action role of the contemporary domestic garden. Traditionally, the spaces between the low hedges were filled with different coloured gravel, sand, coal and even glass, and only in comparatively recent times has planting been used.

Mazes are features on the grand scale, designed with a glorious sense of humour and with the express intention of making participants lose their way within the design. Hedges are normally used to outline the pattern, with yew as the first choice,

Although many parterres have historical connotations, they can be used in gardens of any period, whether classic or contemporary. Establishing them is also relatively quick.

Here, the two colours of the different species of box have been trained to swoop over and under one another to great dramatic effect, forming a traditional knot pattern.

Mazes come in all shapes and sizes, and can be either formal or informal, but this pattern is gloriously organic in conception and outline. There is an enormous feeling of

rhythm and movement here which can be best appreciated from higher ground. Such an aspect also allows a viewer to shout instructions to anyone lost in the maze!

and holly, which discourages cutting corners, running a close second. Hedges were not always above eye level, and mazes can also be created from a pattern of paths, or simply mown out of a lawn, when willpower will play its part!

Uses: Although parterres were designed for grand gardens, the formula can easily be reworked in a simpler form to fit into a smaller plot. Small, ornamental beds of geometric design can be edged with low-growing plants and filled with a bold planting of a few or even a single species, or, in the traditional way, with different gravels. Bulbs followed by summer bedding is rigidly effective; box hedging filled with clipped santolina is stunning; and herbs and vegetables can also be used to form parterres. If you have the space, a hedged maze is always a possibility, but even a mown maze in the rougher grass of an orchard will give pleasure. Once you tire of it, you can change the pattern – or do away with it entirely.

Planting: Some of the best plants for edging parterres or knots include the small-leafed box, *Lonicera nitida*, *Berberis thunbergii* 'Atropurpurea Nana' and lavender. Fillers could include Dutch lavender, dwarf santolina, and bedding plants in a single colour.

Mazes can take a bolder material, such as yew, holly, beech and hornbeam. None of these is fussy about soil, but, as it is for all hedges, good preparation is important. A maze is clipped in exactly the same way as a normal hedge.

Contrasting & associating materials: Such features are essentially set pieces, and will look happiest within the geometry and amidst the natural materials of a traditional formal garden: natural stone, brick, gravel or grass paths and sweeping lawns. However, there is no reason why such features should not be brought up to date, using crisp geometry and hi-tech materials. How about a maze in contrasting colours of Astroturf, or, even more off-beat, one constructed from acrylic mirror walls? Get out of that one!

Purple and grey is always a sound colour combination, especially when contained, as here, within a sweeping parterre edged with box and divided by carefully tended gravel paths. The secret of planting in such compositions is to choose species that will not outgrow their allotted positions, thereby engulfing the dominant framework of hedging.

LARGE-SCALE AVENUES

This avenue, with its delicate cherry trees drawing the eye down towards the statue, would be relatively simple to duplicate in a medium-sized garden. Although the trees are attractively underplanted, this does not detract from the overall concept.

Characteristics: The purpose of an avenue is to heighten tension and lead the eye forward to focus on a major feature, usually the house but sometimes an incidental feature such as a pool, substantial garden building, or a fine view. An avenue on a grand scale requires space, integrity of design and, above all, respect. This is not a device to be reproduced half-heartedly; it is all or nothing, and a row of scraggy cherries set in too small a plot in front of a pseudo-mansion lacks the style that an avenue deserves.

Avenues on a grand scale demand forest trees. Oak, chestnut, lime and beech can all be used, and their regular outlines will add to the drama. The lower branches will be pruned automatically if stock are present, giving the trees an absolutely horizontal bottom edge. Fastigiate Lombardy poplars provide vertical emphasis, as well as tension at ground level, and form a dominant punctuation point from a distance. Unlike many other species, they are quick to establish themselves, although relatively short-lived.

Uses: There are two major ways in which grand avenues are used: those flanking a driveway are primarily concerned with the approach to the house; others radiate away from the building, out into the landscape or towards a subsidiary feature. Apart from cross-axes, views to either side of an avenue should be discouraged, and the wide expanse of empty parkland through which such avenues often run, helps to add emphasis to the avenue itself.

Planting: A single avenue is superb, but a double avenue, where space permits, can look even more stunning. Avenues normally consist of repeat planting of the same species, and as a general rule, trees should be planted at least the distance of their eventual height away from a drive. Upright Lombardy poplars will be planted about 7m (20ft) apart while beech or chestnut will be spaced at about twice that distance. Stout stakes and tree guards are essential to prevent wind damage and possible attack by livestock.

Designers sometimes play around with false perspective, narrowing the avenue towards the focal point in order to achieve an impression of greater distance. While this might work from the main viewpoint, it looks distinctly odd from the other end. So I would not recommend doing it. Remember, you are planting for future generations – a rare and wonderful thing to be doing.

Contrasting & associating materials: Surrounding parkland and a gravel driveway are the least and the most that you will need; leave it at that!

Not all avenues need to be straight; here there is a real feeling of movement and mystery as the curving line of trees and mown grass draws you onwards. The rougher grass allowed to grow to its natural height provides just the right degree of delineation, but at the same time allows glimpses of the view to either side.

SMALL-SCALE AVENUES

Hostas are among the most architectural of garden plants. In this composition they are backed by a sombre avenue of young trees to provide great continuity. Notice how the white bench reflects the light back up the path; a darker colour would be far less effective.

Characteristics: The same principle of drawing the eye to a focal point (house, pool, statue, summerhouse, seat, or other garden feature) can be adopted in a more intimate situation by using a regularly planted succession of clipped shrubs, or clipped or pleached small trees.

It is also essential that an avenue leads somewhere, and that once arrived at, the view back from a focal point is as strong as the view towards it. There is little point in arriving at a delightful summerhouse, only to turn round and have the eye led to the back of someone's garage – avenue or no avenue! Although usually planted, much the same effect can be achieved by using flanking posts and ropes, perhaps interspersed with small trees or lower planting.

Uses: Smaller avenues follow the same principles as large ones, but on a smaller scale. They often look best in a formal layout, and can be set within or contained by planting on either side, which will prevent the view from leaking out into other parts of the garden. An avenue can be a powerful device for drawing the eye away from a poor view, but the smaller the garden, the more careful you have to be to prevent it from dominating everything else.

Planting: Yews, clipped into a series of regular shapes, form some of the best small avenues, but some of the neater medium-height conifers also come into their own. Pleached trees are perfect for this scale of avenue, and can form a powerful and dramatic garden feature. Lime and hornbeam are ideal for this kind of high-level hedge, with their upper branches tied into wires to flank the avenue, and their stems left clean. They need careful pruning. Avenues, particularly those on a small scale, can have a modern treatment as well as a traditional one. Try using architectural plants such as *Phormium*, yucca or *Cordyline* to flank a crisp, contemporary path.

In all cases, straightforward but thorough soil preparation will be required. When planting, you should remember that the closer plants are positioned, the greater will be the feeling of tension.

Contrasting & associating materials: Smaller avenues such as these relate more intimately to features and materials around them than avenues on a grander scale. A formal setting is usually best, but small-scale avenues set within subtly graded and colour-themed planting can be delightful. All will look superb in a situation where they are associated with traditional materials such as gravel, brick, grass, or natural stone paths.

PLEACHING TREES
Trees such as lime and hornbeam are ideal for pleaching. Carefully prune and train individual branches to horizontal wires stretched tightly between regularly spaced posts.

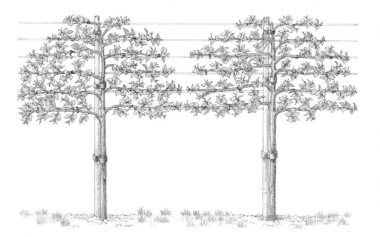

Pleached trees provide high drama and considerable tension as you move between them. The narrower the avenue, the greater the visual restriction, which in turn accelerates the view and often the speed at which you negotiate the walk.

MOVEABLE AVENUES

Instant colour, provided by cheerfully coloured annuals, can brighten an otherwise uninspiring scene. Without such a lift, the mid-green clipped box and dark brickwork of the steps, path and house in this composition would make a sombre scene.

Characteristics: This is the smallest end of the avenue scale, and can work perfectly in even the tiniest garden. The rules are the same, though the lower the feature, the more the eye is drawn down to ground level, emphasizing the surrounding area. Moveable pots and containers trace their pedigree back to the 'Versailles' tubs used on the terraces and paths of the French palace. As with avenue trees, greater continuity and visual pulling power is achieved if the pots used are all of a kind, or at least used in repeated sequence. Planting is a question of choice. Clipped shapes engender greater formality than looser ones, but both are possible candidates; evergreens or evergreys can be used, or an entire range of flowering plants, from shrubs to annuals (remembering that cool colours are relaxing, and hot tones draw the eye); while tender exotics (moved indoors or discarded in winter) will give a tropical feel.

Uses: Moveable pots can be used to create mini avenues and vistas, even on a rotational basis, in different parts of the garden, and can form an integral part of the overall design, whether along paved or mown paths, flanking a lawn or terrace or reinforcing the line of a pergola. Planting can help to influence the formality or informality of the garden, while colours can be used to draw the eye through space. (Remember, if you mix colours in your avenue, to keep the hot tones, such as red, orange and yellow, closest to the main viewpoint, leaving cooler ones in the distance.)

Contrasting & associating materials: Bright, contemporary plastic or fibreglass pots look terrific in a modern setting; terracotta is comfortable nearly everywhere; wooden tubs can be either painted or treated with preservative; stone pots look best in a formal garden.

ACKNOWLEDGEMENTS

The publisher would like to thank the following photographers and organizations for their kind permission to reproduce the photographs in this book.

1 Ron Sutherland/Garden Picture Library (Designer: Anthony Paul); 3 left Clive Nichols(HMP Leyhill); 3 right Gary Rogers/Garden Picture Library; 4 S&O Mathews; 5 above Jerry Harpur (Designer: Isabelle C. Green, Santa Barbara, CA); 5 below Jerry Harpur (Designer: Claus Scheinert); 6 above Marianne Majerus; 6 below Andrew Lawson (Batsford Park, Glos.); 7 left Jerry Harpur ('Ohinetahi', Christchurch, NZ); 7 right Clive Nichols (Bonita Bulaitis, Hampton Court' 96); 8 John Glover (Hiroshi Nanatori); 9 above Jerry Harpur (Designer: Mel Light, LA); 9 below Gary Rogers; 10 Marianne Majerus (Heale House); 10 Andrew Lawson; 11 Andrew Lawson (Gothic House, Oxfordshire);12 Gary Rogers; 12 Brigitte Thomas; 13 left Jerry Harpur ('Dolwen' Cefn Coch, Llanrhaeder-ym-Mochnant.); 13 right Jerry Harpur (Villa Taylor, Marrakech); 14 Charles Mann (John Suarez, Andre Landscape Architects, Scottsdale, AZ); 15 left Christian Sarramon; 15 right Lanny Provo (Buddhist Monastery, Kyoto, Japan); 16 Jerry Harpur (Berry's Garden Company); 17 Andrew Lawson (Thuya Gardens, Maine); 18 Gary Rogers; 19 Jerry Harpur (Oehme and van Sweden Associates, Washington D.C.); 19 Marianne Majerus; 20 Michele Lamontagne; 21 Clive Nichols (Designer: Lucy Gent); 22 left The Garden Picture Library; 22 right Gary Rogers/Andrew Lawson (RHS Gardens Wisley); 23 left Andrew Lawson (Courtesy of Beth Straus); 23 right Andrew Lawson (Designer: Bill Frederick); 24 VTWonen; 25 left Jerry Harpur (Designer: Mark Rumary, Yoxford, Suffolk); 25 right Jerry Harpur (Designer: Sonny Garcia, San Francisco, CA);26 Lanny Provo (West End, Tortola, Virgin Islands); 27 left Clive Nichols (Designer: Jill Billington); 27 right Charles Mann (David Alford, Don Gaspar Compound B&B, Santa Fe, NM); 28 left Vincent Motte; 28 right Jerry Harpur (Designer: Keeyla Meadows, San Francisco, CA); 29 left Paul Ryan/International Interiors; 29 right Brigitte Thomas; 30 Jerry Harpur (Designer: Mel Light, Los Angeles, CA); 31 left Gary Rogers; 31 right Jerry Harpur (Designer: Thomasina Tarling); 32 Jerry Harpur (Ann Griot, LA); 33 left Andrew Lawson; 33 right Jerry Harpur (Designer: Helen Yemm, London); 33 centre Andrew Lawson (Designer: Rupert Golby); 34 Christian Sarramon; 35 S & O Mathews; 35 Andrew Lawson (Courtesy of Lynden B. Miller); 36 Mick Hales (Dr Beisenkamp); 37 Brigitte Thomas/The Garden Picture Library; 37 Charles Mann; 38 Ron Sutherland/Garden Picture Library; 39 above Gary Rogers; 39 below Charles Mann (Designer: Julia Berman, Eden Landscapes, Santa Fe, NM); 40 Annette Schreiner (Designer: F. Bonnin); 41 left Edifice; 41 right Jacqui Hurst; 42 Brigitte Thomas; 43 left Gary Rogers; 43 right Mark Fiennes; 44 Christine Ternynck; 45 Neil Campbell-Sharp; 46 Edifice; 46 Lanny Provo (Owner: Dennis Jenkins, Coconut Grove, Florida.) ; 47 Charles Mann; 48 left Jerry Harpur (Designer: Isabelle C. Green, Santa Barbara.); 48 right Charles Mann (Steve Martino, Martino & Associates, Phoenix, AZ.); 49 left Lanny Provo; 49 right Lanny Provo (Coconut Grove, Florida); 50 Jerry Harpur; 51 Jerry Harpur (Designer: Mel Light, Los Angeles, CA); 51 Edifice; 52 Jerry Harpur (Berry's Garden Company); 53 Marianne Majerus; 53 Mise au Point; 54 left Wildlife Matters; 54 right Clive Nichols (Designer: Sylvia Landsberg, Tudor Knot Garden, Southampton); 55 left Charles Mann (Mike Shoup, Antique Rose Emporium, Brennham, TX); 55 right Jerry Harpur/Elizabeth Whiting & Associates (Gail Jenkins, Melbourne, Victoria); 56 left Charles Mann; 56 right Steven Wooster/The Garden Picture Library (Designers: Duane Paul Design Team); 57 S & O Mathews; 57 Andrew Lawson; 57 left Marijke Heuff/The Garden Picture Library; 58 left S & O Mathews; 58 right Brigitte Thomas; 59 left Jerry Harpur (Michael Wayman, Pymble, NSW); 59 right Gary Rogers; 60 left Edifice; 60 right Gary Rogers/The Garden Picture Library; 61 Barbara Hunt (Designer: Barbara Hunt); 62 Edifice; 63 Gary Rogers; 64 left Edifice; 64 right Edifice; 65 left Charles Mann (Suzanne Crayson, Tesuque Meadows, Santa Fe, NM); 65 right Andrew Lawson; 66 Marianne Majerus (Woodpeckers); 67 Gary Rogers; 68 Christine Ternynck; 69 Neil Campbell-Sharp; 70 S & O Mathews; 70 Brigitte Thomas; 71 left Brigitte Thomas (Easgrove); 71 right Tim Griffiths/The Garden Picture Library; 72 Andrew Lawson (Glendurgan, Cornwall); 72 Marianne Majerus (Woodpeckers); 73 Brigitte Thomas; 74 Jerry Harpur ('Bolobek', Macedon, Australia); 75 Brigitte Thomas; 76 Brigitte Thomas (Hadsbeu); 77 left Gary Rogers; 77 right Charles Mann.